Great Americana

Oregon

John B. Wyeth

Oregon

by John B. Wyeth

READEX MICROPRINT

Foreword

Many persons who went West paid a high penalty
for their ignorance of the country. Such was the experience of John B. Wyeth, who, with a small party of
fellow New Englanders, left Boston in March, 1832, on
a trading and hunting expedition bound for the mouth
of the Columbia River. Less than five months later
Wyeth and six other members of the group found prog-
ress in the Rocky Mountains so painful that they preferred to retrace their steps rather than to continue
through the 400 miles of difficult terrain which still
separated them from the Pacific Ocean. The following
year, 1833, Wyeth published an account of the trip
under the title *Oregon; Or A Short History Of A Long
Journey From The Atlantic Ocean To The Region Of
The Pacific, By Land.*

Wyeth's kinsman, Captain Nathaniel Wyeth, headed
the expedition. Fired by the enthusiastic descriptions
of Oregon by Hall J. Kelly (who had never been there)
and by other writers, Captain Wyeth had assembled a
group to proceed overland for rendezvous on the Pacific
coast with a ship which was to bring supplies around
the Horn. The overland journey went smoothly enough,

at least as far as St. Louis. But after having left St. Louis, the Captain and his men began to realize how little they knew about the West. Every day brought to light some new deficiency in their preparations. The heavy ironware they had brought along for trading purposes greatly impeded their advance. They were only relieved of the burden when a raft loaded with these and other goods capsized in the middle of a river they were trying to cross. Happily they fell in with a group of trappers headed in the same direction before they had gone very far up the Missouri River. It was fortunate that they did, for they might otherwise have perished if left to their own resources. As it was, many of the Captain's party fell ill, and all suffered from lack of food.

For John Wyeth and several others who refused to go farther with the Captain than the Rocky Mountains, the trip home was in some respects more eventful than the journey West. Without money, young Wyeth was reduced to a desperate hand-to-mouth existence even after he reached the Mississippi. For a time he supported himself in plague-ridden New Orleans as a grave digger at two dollars a day. He was compelled to remain there for nine weeks before at last he obtained passage on a ship sailing for Boston.

Once home, Wyeth wrote of his experiences in the West in order that others might learn from his mistakes. He considered it a "sacred cause of humanity... to disabuse the people dwelling on these Atlantic shores respecting the Oregon paradise, lest our farmers' sons and young mechanics should...stray from home, and go they know not whither,—to seek they know not what."

Later, when Captain Wyeth returned to Boston, he was greatly annoyed by his cousin's account of the trip. He pronounced the book "full of white lies." Although the expedition had not been a financial success (the supply ship struck a reef and sank in the Pacific), Captain Wyeth had reached the Pacific coast as planned. Still enthusiastic about the West in spite of everything, Captain Wyeth led a second expedition to the Pacific in 1834.

Reuben G. Thwaites provides an introduction to John Wyeth's book in *Early Western Travels 1748-1846* (Cleveland, 1905), XXI, 9-15. A biography of Captain Wyeth is included in the *Dictionary of American Biography*.

OREGON.

OREGON;

OR

A SHORT HISTORY OF A LONG JOURNEY

FROM THE

ATLANTIC OCEAN TO THE REGION OF THE PACIFIC,

BY LAND;

DRAWN UP FROM THE NOTES AND ORAL INFORMATION

OF

JOHN B. WYETH,

ONE OF THE PARTY WHO LEFT MR. NATHANIEL J. WYETH,

JULY 28TH, 1832, FOUR DAYS' MARCH BEYOND THE RIDGE OF THE

ROCKY MOUNTAINS,

AND THE ONLY ONE WHO HAS RETURNED TO NEW ENGLAND.

———————

CAMBRIDGE:

PRINTED FOR JOHN B. WYETH.

1833.

A CONTENTED MIND IS A CONTINUAL FEAST ; but *entire satisfaction* has never been procured by wealth however enormous, or ambition however successful.

> True happiness is to no place confin'd,
> But still is found in a *contented* mind.

OREGON EXPEDITION.

In order to understand this Oregon Expedition, it is necessary to say, that thirty years ago (1803), PRESIDENT JEFFERSON recommended to Congress to authorize competent officers to explore the river *Missouri* from its mouth to its source, and by crossing the mountains to seek the best water communication thence to the *Pacific* Ocean. This arduous task was undertaken by Captain M. Lewis and Lieutenant W. Clarke of the first regiment of infantry. They were accompanied by a select party of soldiers, and arrived at the Missouri in May, 1804, and persisted in their novel and difficult task into the year 1806, and with such success as to draw from President Jefferson the following testimonial of their heroic services, viz. "The expedition of Messrs. LEWIS & CLARKE, for exploring the river Missouri, and the best communication from that to the *Pacific Ocean*, has had all the success which could be expected ; and for which arduous service they deserve well of their country."

The object of this enterprise was to confer in a friendly manner with the Indian Nations throughout their whole journey, with a view to establish a friendly and equitable commerce with them, on

1

principles emulating those that marked and dignified the settlement of Pennsylvania by *William
Penn*. It was beyond doubt that the President
and Congress sincerely desired to treat the Indians
with kindness and justice, and to establish peace,
order, and good neighbourhood with all the savage
tribes with whom they came in contact, and not
to carry war or violence among any of them who
appeared peaceably disposed.

A few years before the period of which we have
spoken, our government had acquired by purchase
the vast and valuable Territory of Louisiana from
the renowned NAPOLEON BONAPARTE, at that time
the Chief of the French Nation.   Considering his
previous intentions, and actual preparations under
his famous General *Bernadotte*, nothing could be
more fortunate for these United States than this
purchase.   Our possession of Louisiana was so
grievous a sore to the very jealous Spaniards, that
they have, till lately, done all in their power to debar and mislead us from pursuing discoveries in that
quarter, or in the Arkansas, Missouri, or *Oregon*.
Yet few or none of them probably believed that
we should, during the present generation, or the
next, attempt the exploration of the distant *Oregon*
Territory, which extends from the *Rocky Mountains* to the shores of the Pacific Ocean, or in other
words, from the Missouri and Yellow Stone rivers
to that of the river Columbia or Oregon which
pours into the Ocean by a wide mouth at the immense distance from us of about four thousand
miles; yet one and twenty men, chiefly farmers
and a few mechanics had the hardihood to undertake it, and that too with deliberation and sober
calculation.   But what will not a New-England

man undertake when honor and interest are the objects before him ? Have not the people of that
sand-bank, Nantucket, redeemed it from the ocean,
and sailed round Cape Horn in pursuit of whales
for their oil, and seals for their skins ? A score of
our farmers seeing that Nantucket and New Bed-
ford had acquired riches and independence by
traversing the sea to the distant shores of the Pacific, determined to do something like it *by land.*
Their ardor seemed to have hidden from their eyes
the mighty difference between the facility of passing in a ship with the aid of sails, progressing
day and night, by skilfully managing the winds
and the helm, and that of a complicated wagon
upon wheels, their journey to be over mountains and rivers, and through hostile tribes of
savages who dreaded and hated the sight of a
white man.

This novel expedition was not however the original
or spontaneous notion of Mr. Nathaniel J. Wyeth,
nor was it entirely owing to the publications of
Lewis & Clarke or Mackenzie. Nor was it entirely owing to the enterprise of Messrs. Barrell,
Hatch, and Bulfinch, who fitted out two vessels
that sailed from Boston in 1787, commanded by Captains Kendrick and Gray, which vessels arrived at
Nootka in September, 1788. They were roused to
it by the writings of Mr. Hall J. Kelly, who had
read all the books he could get on the voyages and
travels in Asia, Africa, Europe, and America, until
he had heated his mind to a degree little short of
the valorous Knight of La Mancha, that is to say,
he believed all he read, and was firm in the opinion
that an Englishman and an American, or either,
by himself, could endure and achieve any thing

that any man could do with the same help, and
farther, that a New-England man or "Yankee,"
could with less. That vast region, which stretches
from between the east of the Mississippi, and south
of the Lakes *Superior, Huron, Michigan, Erie,*
and *Ontario,* was too narrow a space for the enterprise of men born and bred within a mile or two
of the oldest University in the United States.
Whatever be the true character of the natives of
New England, one thing must be allowed them,
that of great and expansive ideas, — beyond, far
beyond the generality of the inhabitants of the
small Island of Britain. I say small, for if that
Island should be placed in the midst of these United
States, it would hardly form more than a single mem-
ber of our extended republic. That vast rivers,
enormous mountains, tremendous cataracts, with
an extent corresponding to the hugeness of the fea-
tures of America, naturally inspire men with bound-
less ideas, few will doubt. This adventurous disposition, at the same time, will as naturally banish
from the mind what the *new-light* doctrine of Phre-
nology calls the disposition bump of *Inhabitiveness,*
or an inclination to stay at home, and in its place give
rise to a roaming, wandering inclination, which, some
how or other, may so affect the organs of vision, and
of hearing, as to debar a person from perceiving what
others may see, the innumerable difficulties in the
way. Mr. Hall J. Kelly's writings operated like a
match applied to the combustible matter accumula-
ted in the mind of the energetic Nathaniel J. Wyeth,
which reflected and multiplied the flattering glass
held up to view by the ingenious and well-disposed
schoolmaster.

Mr. Nathaniel J. Wyeth had listened with peculiar

delight to all the flattering accounts from the Western regions, and that at a time when he was surrounded with apparent advantages, and even enviable circumstances. He was born and bred near the borders of a beautiful small Lake, as it would be called in Great Britain; but what we in this country call a large Pond; because we generally give the name of Lakes only to our vast inland seas, some of which almost rival in size the Caspian and Euxine in the old world. It seems that he gave entire credit to the stories of the wonderful fertility of the soil on the borders of the Ohio, Missouri, the river Platte, and the Oregon, with the equally wonderful healthfulness of the climate. We need not wonder that a mind naturally ardent and enterprising should become too enthusiastic to pursue the laborious routine of breaking up and harrowing the hard and stubborn soil of Massachusetts within four miles of the sea, where the shores are bounded and fortified by stones and rocks, which extend inland, lying just below the surface of the ground, while the regions of the West were represented as standing in need of very little laborious culture, such was the native vigor of its black soil. The spot where our adventurer was born and grew up, had many peculiar and desirable advantages over most others in the county of Middlesex. Besides rich pasturage, numerous dairies, and profitable orchards, and other fruit trees, it possessed the luxuries of well cultivated gardens of all sorts of culinary vegetables, and all within three miles of the Boston Market-House, and two miles of the largest live-cattle market in New England. All this, and more too, had not sufficient attractions to retain Mr. Wyeth in his native town and county.

1*

Beside these blessings, I shall add another.
The Lake I spoke of, commonly called *Fresh
Pond*, is a body of delightful water, which seems
to be the natural head or source of all the numerous underground rivers running between it and the
National Navy Yard at Charlestown, which is so
near to the city of Boston as to be connected to it
by a bridge ; for wherever you sink a well, between
the body of water just mentioned, you strike a pel-
lucid vein of it at from nineteen to twenty-two
feet depth from the surface. With the aforesaid
Lake or Pond is connected another not quite so
large, but equally beautiful. Around these bodies
of inosculating waters, are well cultivated farms
and a number of gentlemen's country-seats, forming a picture of rural beauty and plenty not easily
surpassed in Spring, Summer, and Autumn ; and
when winter has frozen the lakes and all the rivers,
this spot has another and singular advantage ; for
our adventurer sold the *water* of this pond ; which
was sent to the West-India Islands, Philadelphia,
New Orleans, and other places south of this ; which
is so much of a singularity as to require explana-
tion.

In our very coldest weather, January and February, the body of water we spoke of is almost
every year frozen to the thickness of from eighteen
inches to two feet, — sometimes less, and very rarely more. It is then sawed into cubes of the size
just mentioned, and deposited in large store-houses,
and carted thence every month in the year, even
through the dog-days, in heavy teams drawn by
oxen and horses to the wharves in Boston, and
put on board large and properly constructed vessels, and carried into the hot climates already

mentioned. The heavy teams five, or six, or more, close following each other, day and night, and even through the hottest months, would appear incredible to a stranger. Here was a traffic without any drawback, attended with no other charge than the labor of cutting and transporting the article ; for the pond belonged to no man, any more than the air which hung above it. Both belonged to mankind. No one claimed any personal property in it, or control over it from border to border. A clearer profit can hardly be imagined. While the farmer was ploughing his ground, manuring and planting it, securing his well-tended crop by fencing, and yet after all his labor, the Hessian-fly, the canker or slug worm, or some other destructive insect, or some untimely frost, as was the case last winter, might lay waste all his pains and cut off all his expectations. The only risk to which the Ice-merchant was liable was a blessing to most of the community ; I mean the mildness of a winter that should prevent his native lake from freezing a foot or two thick. Our fishermen have a great advantage over the farmer in being exempt from fencing, walling, manuring, taxation, and dry seasons ; and only need the expence of a boat, line, and hook, and the risk of life and health ; but from all these the Ice-man is in a manner entirely exempted ; and yet the Captain of this Oregon Expedition seemed to say, All this availeth me nothing, so long as I read books in which I find, that by only going about *four thousand miles*, over land, from the shore of our *Atlantic* to the shore of the *Pacific*, after we have there entrapped and killed the beavers and otters, we shall be able, after building vessels for the purpose, to carry our most valuable peltry to China and Cochin China, our seal-skins to Japan, and our superfluous grain to various Asiatic ports, and lumber to the Spanish settlements on the Pacific; and to become rich by underworking and underselling the people of Hindostan; and, to crown all, to extend far and wide the traffic in oil by killing tame whales on the spot, instead of sailing round the stormy region of Cape Horn.

All these advantages and more too were suggested to divers discontented and impatient young men. Talk to them of the great labor, toil, and risk, and they would turn a deaf ear to you: argue with them, and you might as well reason with a snow-storm. Enterprising young men run away with the idea that *the farther they go from home, the surer they will be of making a fortune.* The original projector of this golden vision first talked himself into the visionary scheme, and then talked twenty others into the same notion. Some of their neighbours and well-wishers thought differently from them; and some of the oldest, and most thoughtful, and prudent endeavoured to dissuade them from so very arduous and hazardous an expedition. But young and single men are for tempting the untried scene; and when either sex has got a notion of that sort, the more you try to dissuade them, the more intent they are on their object. Nor is this bent of mind always to be censured, or wondered at. Were every man to be contented to remain in the town in which he was born, and to follow the trade of his father, there would be an end to improvement, and a serious impediment to spreading population. It is difficult to draw the exact line between contentment, and that inactivity which approaches laziness. The disposition either way seems stamped upon us by *nature*, and therefore innate. This is certainly the case with birds and beasts; — the wild geese emigrate late in the Autumn to a southern climate, and return again in the Spring to a northern one, while the owl and several other birds remain all their lives near where they were hatched; whereas man is not so much confined by a natural bias to his native home. He can live in all climates from the equator to very near the dreary poles, which is not the case with other animals; and it would seem that nature intended he should live any where; — for whereas other animals are restricted in their articles of food, some living wholly on flesh, and others wholly on vegetables, man is capable of feeding upon every thing that is eatable by any creature, and of mixing every article together, and varying them by his knowledge and art of cookery, — a knowledge and skill belonging to man alone. Hence it appears that *Providence*, who directs every thing for the best, intended that man should wander over the globe, inhabit every region, and dwell wherever the sun could shine upon him, and where water could be obtained for his use.

So far from deriding the disposition to explore unknown regions, we should consider judicious travellers as so many benefactors of mankind. It is most commonly a propensity that marks a vigorous intellect, and a benevolent heart. The conduct of the Spaniards, when they conquered Mexico and Peru with the sole view of robbing them of their gold and silver, and of forcing them to abandon their native religion, has cast an odium on those first adventurers upon this continent and their first enterprises in India have stigmatized the Dutch and the English; nor were our own forefathers, who left England to enjoy religious freedom, entirely free from the stain of injustice and cruelty towards the native Indians. — Let us therefore in charity, nay, in justice, speak cautiously of what may seem to us censurable in the first explorers of uncivilized countries; and if we should err in judgment, let it be on the side of commendation.

Mr. Wyeth, or as we shall hereafter call him, *Captain* Wyeth, as being leader of the Band of the Oregon adventurers, after having inspired twenty-one persons with his own high hopes and expectations (among whom was his own brother, Dr. Jacob Wyeth, and a gun-smith, a black-smith, two carpenters, and two fishermen, the rest being farmers and laborers, brought up to no particular trade) was ready, with his companions, to start off to the Pacific Ocean, the first of March, 1832, to go from Boston to the mouth of Columbia river by land.

I was the youngest of the company, not having attained my twentieth year; but, in the plenitude of health and spirits, I hoped every thing, believed every thing my kinsman, the Captain, believed and said, and all doubts and fears were banished. The Captain used to convene us every Saturday night at his house for many months previous to our departure, to arrange and settle the plan of our future movements, and to make every needful preparation; and such were his thoughtfulness and vigilance, that it seemed to us nothing was forgotten and every thing necessary provided. Our three vehicles, or wagons, if we may call by that name a *unique* contrivance, half boat, and half carriage, may be mentioned as an instance of our Captain's talents for snug contrivance.   It was a boat of about thirteen feet long, and four feet wide, of a shape partly of a canoe, and partly of a gondola, It was not calked with tarred oakum, and payed with pitch, lest the rays of the sun should injure it while upon wheels ; but it was nicely jointed, and dovetailed.   The boat part was firmly connected with the lower, or axletree, or wheel part ; — the whole was so constructed that the four wheels of it were to be taken off when we came to a river, and placed in the wagon, while the tongue or shaft was to be towed across by a rope.   Every thing was as light as could be consistent with safety. Some of the Cambridge wags said it was a boat begot upon a wagon, — a sort of mule, neither horse nor ass, — a mongrel, or as one of the collegians said it was a thing *amphibious*, anatomically constructed like some equivocal animals, allowing it to crawl upon the land, or to swim on the water ; and he therefore thought it ought to be denominated an *amphibium*.   This would have gone off very well, and to the credit of the learned collegian, had not one of the gang, who could hardly write his own name, demurred at it ; because he said that it reflected not back the honor due to the ingenious contriver of the commodious and truly original vehicle ; and for his part, he thought that if they meant to give it a particular name, that should redound to the glory of the inventor, it ought to be called a *Nat-wyethium ;* and this was instantaneously agreed to by acclamation !   Be that as it may, the vehicle did not disgrace the inventive genius of New England.   This good-humored raillery, shows the opinion of indifferent people, merely lookers-on.   The fact was, the generality

of the people in Cambridge considered it a hazardous enterprise, and considerably notional. About
this time there appeared some well written essays
in the Boston newspapers, to show the difficulty
and impracticability of the scheme, purporting to
doubt the assertions of Mr. Hall J. Kelly respecting the value and pleasantness of the Oregon territory. The three vehicles contained a gross of axes,
a variety of articles, or "*goods*" so called, calculated for the Indian market, among which vermilion and other paints were not forgotten, glass
beads, small looking-glasses, and a number of tawdry trinkets, cheap knives, buttons, nails, hammers,
and a deal of those articles, on which young Indians
of both sexes set a high value, and white men little
or none. Such is the spirit of trade and traffic,
from the London and Amsterdam merchant, down
to an Indian trader and a yankee tin-ware man in
his jingling go-cart; in which he travels through
Virginia and the Carolinas to vend his wares,
and cheat the Southerners, and bring home laugha-
ble anecdotes of their simplicity and ignorance, to
the temporary disgrace of the common people of
the Northern and Eastern part of the Union, where
a travelling tin-man dare hardly show himself, —
and yet is held up in the South as the real New-
England character, and this by certain white people who know the use of letters!

The company were uniform in their dress. Each
one wore a coarse woollen jacket and pantaloons, a
striped cotton shirt, and cowhide boots: every man
had a musket, most of them rifles, all of them
bayonets in a broad belt, together with a large
clasped knife for eating and common purposes. The
Captain and one or two more added pistols; but

every one had in his belt a small axe. This uniformity had a pleasing effect, which, together with their curious wagons, was noticed with commendation in the Baltimore newspapers, as a striking contrast with the family emigrants of husband, wife, and children, who have for thirty years and more passed on to the Ohio, Kentucky, and other territories. The whole bore an aspect of energy, good contrivance, and competent means. I forgot to mention that we carried tents, camp-kettles, and the common utensils for cooking victuals, as our plan was to live like soldiers, and to avoid, as much as possible, inns and taverns.

The real and avowed object of this hardy-looking enterprise was to go to the river Columbia, otherwise called the river *Oregon*, or river of the *West*, which empties by a very wide mouth into the Pacific Ocean, and there and thereabouts commence a fur trade by trafficking with the Indians, as well as beaver and other hunting by ourselves. We went upon shares, and each one paid down so much; and our association was to last during five years. Each man paid our Leader forty dollars. Captain Wyeth was our Treasurer, as well as Commander; and all the expenses of our travelling on wheels, and by water in steam-boats, were defrayed by our Leader, to whom we all promised fidelity and obedience. For twenty free-born New-England men, brought up in a sort of Indian freedom, to be bound together to obey a leader in all things reasonable, without something like *articles of war*, was, to say the least of it, a hazardous experiment. The Captain and crew of a Nantucket whaling ship come nearest to such an association; for in this case each man runs that great risk of his life, in voluntarily attacking and killing a whale, which could not be expected from men hired by the day, like soldiers; so much stronger does association for gain operate, than ordinary wages. As fighting Indians from behind trees and rocks is, next in point of courage, to attacking a whale, the monarch of the main, in his own element, a common partnership is the only scheme for achieving and securing such dangerous purposes.

We left the city of Boston, 1st of March, 1832, and encamped on one of the numerous islands in its picturesque harbour, where we remained ten days, by way of inuring ourselves to the tented field; and on the 11th of the same month we hoisted sail for Baltimore, where we arrived after a passage of fifteen days, not without experiencing a snow-storm, severe cold, and what the landsmen considered a hard gale, at which I, who had been one voyage to sea, did not wonder. It made every man on board look serious; and glad were we to be set on shore at the fair city of Baltimore, in which are to be found a great number of merchants, traders, and mechanics from different parts of New England, and where of course there are none, or very few, of those ridiculous prejudices against what they call Yankees, that are observable in Virginia and the Carolinas.

At Baltimore our amphibious carriages excited great attention, and I may add, our whole company was an object of no small curiosity and respect. This, said they, is " *Yankee all over!* " — bold enterprise, neatness, and good contrivance. As we carefully avoided the expense of inns and taverns, we marched two miles out of Baltimore, and there encamped during four days; and then we put our

wagons into the *cars* on the rail-road; which extends from thence sixty miles, which brought us to
the foot of the Alleghany mountains. Quitting the
rail-road at the foot of the Alleghany, we encoun-
tered that mountain. Here we experienced a degree of inhospitality not met with among the savages. The Innkeepers, when they found that we
came from New England, betrayed an unwilling-
ness to accommodate Yankees, from a ridiculous
idea, that the common people, so nicknamed, were
too shrewd at a bargain and trading, for a slow
and straight-forward Dutchman; for the inhabitants of this mountainous region, were generally
sons and grandsons of the Dutch and German
first settlers; and it cannot be denied and concealed,
that the New England land-jobbers were in their
bargains too hard for the torpid Dutchmen, who,
it is true, loved money as much as any people, yet
when they, or their fathers had been the sufferers
from a set of roving sharpers, it is no wonder that
an hereditary prejudice should descend with ex-
aggeration and aggravation from father to son, and
that their resentment should visit their innocent
sons to the third and fourth generation. No one
pretends to mention any fact or deed, in which
those Dutch foreigners were defrauded of their
rights and dues; and all that can be, with truth,
said, was, that the land-speculators from Connecti-
cut and Massachusetts were to New-England
what Yorkshire men are thought to be to the rest
of the people of England, a race more sharp and
quick-sighted than their neighbours, — and with a
sort of constitutional good humor, called *fun*, they
could twist that uneducated progeny of a German
stock around their fingers; — hence their reluctance

to have any thing to do with men, whose grand-fathers were too knowing for them. You never hear the French or the English complaining of the over-shrewdness of the New-England people. They accord very well together, and very frequent-ly intermarry. No, it is the Dutch, and the de-scendants of transported convicts, who sneer at those they call Yankees, whom their fathers feared, and of course hated.

At one public house on the mountains near which we halted, the master of it, learning that we came from Boston, refused us any refreshment and lodg-ing. He locked up his bar-room, put the key in his pocket, went out, and came back with four or five of his neighbours, when the disagreement ran so high, that the tavern-keeper and the Yankee Captain each seized his rifle. The latter pointing to the other's *sign* before his door, demanded both lodging and refreshment, as the legal condition of his tavern-license ; * and the dispute ended in our Captain's sleeping in the house with three of his party, well armed, determined to defend their per-sons, and to insist on their rights as peaceable and unoffending travellers, while the rest of the com-pany bivouacked near their wagons, and reposed themselves, like veteran soldiers, in their tents and wagons.

We gladly departed from the inhospitable Alle-ghany or Apalachian mountains, which extend from the river St. Lawrence to the confines of Georgia,

---

* Taverners are by law to be provided with suitable bedding for travellers. and stables and provisions for horses and cattle. Brownsville is a flourishing town situated on the point, where the great Cumberland road strikes the head of navigation of the Mo-nongahela, and has long been a place of embarkation for emigrants for the West.

and which run nearly parallel to the sea-shore from
sixty to one hundred and thirty miles from it,
and dividing the rivers, which flow into the
Atlantic on the east, from those that run into
the lakes and into the Mississippi on the west.
The part we passed was in the state of Pennsylvania. Our next stretch was for the river Monongahela, where we took the steamboat for *Pittsburg*. This town has grown in size and wealth,
in a few years, surprisingly. It is two hundred
and thirty miles from Baltimore; three hundred
from Philadelphia. It is built on a point of land
jutting out towards the river Ohio, and washed on
each side by the Alleghany and Monongahela,
which rivers uniting are lost in the noble Ohio. It
was originally a fortress built by the French, called
Fort du Quesne; being afterwards taken by the
English in 1759, it was called fort *Pitt*, in honor of
the famous *William Pitt*, afterwards Earl of Chat-
ham, under whose administration it was taken from
the French, together with all Canada. On this
spot a city has been reared by the Americans,
bearing the name of *Pittsburg*, which has thriven
in a surprising manner by its numerous manufactories in glass, as well as in all the metals in common
use. To call it the Birmingham of America is
to underrate its various industry; and to call the
English Birmingham Pittsburg, would be to confer upon that town additional honor; not but what
the British Birmingham is by far the most pleasant
place to live in. Pittsburg is the region of iron
and fossil coal, of furnaces, glass-works, and a
variety of such like manufactures. This town
has somewhat the color of a coal-pit, or of a black-
smith's shop, The wonder is, that any gentleman

2*

of property should ever think of building a costly
dwelling-house, with corresponding furniture, in the
coal region of the western world; but there is no
disputing *de gustibus* — *Chacun à son gout.* The
rivers and the surrounding country are delightful,
and the more so from the contrast between them
and that hornet's nest of bustle and dirt, the rich
capital. Thousands of miserable culprits are doom-
ed to delve in deep mines of silver, gold, and
quicksilver among the Spaniards for their crimes;
but here they are all freemen, who choose to
breathe smoke, and swallow dirt, for the sake of
clean dollars and shining eagles. Hence it is that
the Pittsburgh workmen appear, when their faces
are washed, with the ruddiness of high health, the
plenitude of good spirits, and the confidence of
freemen.

From the busy city of thriving Pittsburg our
next important movement was down the Ohio.
We accordingly embarked in a very large steam-
boat called The Freedom; and soon found ourselves,
bag and baggage very much at our ease and satisfaction, on board a truly wonderful floating inn,
hotel, or tavern, for such are our steam-boats. Nothing of the kind can surpass the beauty of
this winding river, with its fine back-ground
of hills of all shapes and colors, according to the
advancement of vegetation from the shrubs to the
tallest trees. But the romantic scenery on both
sides of the Ohio is so various and so captivat-
ing to a stranger, that it requires the talents of a
painter to give even a faint idea of the picture;
and the effect on my mind was, not to estimate
them as I ought, but to feed my deluded imagination with the belief that we should find on the

Missouri, and on the Rocky Mountains, and Columbia river, objects as much finer than the Ohio
afforded, as this matchless river exceeded our
Merrimac or Kennebeck: and so it is with the
youth of both sexes; not satisfied with the present
gifts of nature, they pant after *the untried scene*,
which imagination is continually bodying forth, and
time as constantly dissipating.

The distance from Pittsburg to the Mississippi
is about one thousand miles.   Hutchins estimated
it at one thousand one hundred and eighty-eight, —
Dr. Drake at only nine hundred and forty-nine.
Wheeling is a town of some importance.   Here
the great national road into the interior from the
city of Washington, meets that of Zanesville,
Chillicothè, Columbus, and Cincinnati.   It is the
best point to aim at in very low stages of the water, and from thence boats may go at all seasons of
the year.   We passed Marietta, distinguished for
its remarkable remains of mounds, and works, resembling modern fortifications, but doubtless the
labor of the ancient aboriginals, of whom there
is now no existing account; but by these works, and
articles found near them, they must have belonged
to a race of men farther advanced in arts and
civilization than the present Indians in that region,
— a people who, we may well suppose, were the
ancestors of the Mexicans.   Yet we see at this
time little more than log-houses belonging to miserable tenants of white people.   All the sugar used
by the people here is obtained from the maple tree.
Fossil coal is found along the banks.   There is a
creek pouring forth *Petroleum*, about one hundred
miles from Pittsburg on the Alleghany, called *Oil*
Creek, which will blaze on the application of a

match. This is not uncommon in countries abounding in bituminous coal. Nitre is found wherever there are suitable caves and caverns for its collection. The people here are rather boisterous in their manners, and intemperate in their habits, by what we saw and heard, more so than on the other side of the river where slavery is prohibited. Indeed slavery carries a black moral mark with it visible on those whose skins are naturally of a different color ; and Mr. Jefferson's opinion of the influence of slavery on the whites, justifies our remark.

We stopped one day and night at the flourishing town of *Cincinnati*, the largest city in the Western country, although laid out so recently as 1788. It is twenty miles above the mouth of the Great Miami, and four hundred and sixty-five miles below Pittsburg. It appears to great advantage from the river, the ground inclining gradually to the water. Three of us had an evidence of that by a mischievous trick for which we deserved punishment. We were staring about the fine city that has risen up with a sort of rapid, mushroom growth, surprising to every one who sees it, and who considers that it is not more than forty years old. In the evening we went into a public house, where we treated ourselves with that sort of refreshment which inspires fun, frolic, and mischief. We remained on shore till so late an hour that every body appeared to have gone to bed, when we set out to return to our steam-boat. In our way to it we passed by a store, in the front of which stood three barrels of lamp-oil, at the head of a fine sloping street. The evil spirit of mischief put it into our heads to set them a rolling down the inclined plane to the river. No sooner hinted, than executed.

We set all three a running, and we ran after them; and what may have been lucky for us, they were recovered next day whole.   Had there been legal inquisition made for them, we had determined to plead *character*, that we were from Boston, the land of steady habits and good principles, and that it must have been some gentlemen Southerners, with whose characters for nightly frolics, we, who lived within sound of the bell of the University of Cambridge were well acquainted.   The owners of the oil came down to the steam-boat, and carried back their property without making a rigid examination for the offenders; without suspecting that prudent New-England young men would indulge in a wanton piece of fun, where so much was at stake.   But John Bull and Jonathan are queer fellows.

From Cincinnati to St. Louis, we experienced some of those disagreeable occurrences, that usually happen to democratical adventurers.   Our Captain, to lessen the expenses of the expedition, had bargained with the Captain of the steam-boat, that we of his band should assist in taking on board wood from the shore, to keep our boilers from cooling. Although every one saw the absolute necessity of the thing, for our common benefit and safety, yet some were for demurring at it, as not previously specified and agreed upon.   Idleness engenders mutiny oftener than want.   In scarcity and in danger men cling together like gregarious animals; but as soon as an enterprising gang can sit down, as in a steamboat, with nothing to do but to find fault, they are sure to become discontented, and discontent indulged leads to mutiny.   Whatever I thought then, I do not think now that Captain Wyeth was to blame for directing his followers to aid in *wooding;* nor should the men have grumbled at it. I now am of opinion that our aiding in wooding the steam-boat was right, reasonable, and proper. Every man of us, except the surgeon of the company, Dr. Jacob Wyeth, ought, on every principle of justice and generosity, to have given that assistance.

Our navigation from Cincinnati to St. Louis was attended with circumstances new, interesting, and very often alarming. Passing the rapids of the Ohio, or *falls* as they are called, between the Indiana territory and Kentucky, was sufficiently appalling to silence all grumbling. These falls, or rapids are in the vicinity of Louisville, Jeffersonville, Clarksville, and Shipping-port, and are really terrific to an inexperienced farmer or mechanic. Our Hell-gate in Long-Island Sound is a common brook compared with them; and when we had passed through them into the Mississippi, the assemblage of trees in the river, constituting snags and sawyers, offered themselves as a species of risk and danger, which none of us had ever calculated on or dreamt of. We knew that there was danger in great storms, of huge trees blowing down on one's head; and that those who took shelter under them in a thunder-storm, risked their lives from lightning; but to meet destruction from trees in an immense river, seemed to us a danger of life, which we had not bargained for, and entirely out of our agreement and calculation. We had braced ourselves up only against the danger of hostile Indians, and enraged beasts, which we meant to war against. Beyond that, all was smooth water to us. The truth of the matter is, —

the men whom Captain Wyeth had collected were not the sort of men for such an expedition. They were too much on an equality to be under strict orders like soldiers. Lewis & Clarke were very fortunate in the men they had under them. Major Long's company was, in a great degree, military, and yet three of his soldiers deserted him at one time, and a fourth soon after.

On the 18th of April, 1832, we arrived at St. Louis. As we had looked forward to this town, as a temporary resting-place, we entered it in high spirits, and pleased ourselves with a notion that the rest of our way till we should come to the Rocky Mountains would be, if not down hill, at least on a level: but we counted without our host.

St. Louis was founded by a Frenchman named *Peter la Clade* in 1764, eighty-four years after the establishment of Fort Crève-cœur on the Illinois river; and inhabited entirely by Frenchmen and the decendants of Frenchmen, who had carried on for the most part a friendly and lucrative trade with the Indians. But since the vast Western country has been transferred to the United States, its population has been rapidly increased by numerous individuals and families from different parts of the Union; and its business extended by enterprising mechanics and merchants from the New-England States; and its wealth greatly augmented. The old part of St. Louis has a very different aspect from that of Cincinnati, where every thing appears neat, and new, and tasteful; as their public buildings, their theatre, and spacious hotels, not forgetting Madam Trollope's bazar, or, as it is commonly called, "Trollope's Folly," as well as its spacious streets, numerous coaches, and other

marks of rapid wealth, and growing luxury. As
St. Louis has advanced in wealth, magnitude, and
importance, it has gradually changed the French
language and manners, and assumed the American.
It however contains, I am told, many of the old
stock that are very respectable for their literary
acquirements and polished manners.

We shall avoid, as we have avowed, any thing
like censure of Captain Wyeth's scheme during his
absence; but when we arrived at St. Louis, we
could not but lament his want of information,
respecting the best means of obtaining the great
objects of our enterprise. Here we were con-
strained to sell our complicated wagons for less
than half what they originally cost. We were
convinced that they were not calculated for the
rough roads, and rapid streams and eddies of some
of the rivers we must necessarily pass. We here
thought of the proverb, "that men never do a thing
right the first time." Captain Wyeth might have
learned at St. Louis, that there were two wealthy
gentlemen who resided at or near that place, who
had long since established a regular trade with the
Indians, Mr. M——, and a young person, Mr. S——,
and that a stranger could hardly compete with such
established traders. The turbulent tribe, called
the *Black-foot* tribe, had long been supplied with
fire arms and ammunition, beads, vermilion and other
paints, tobacco and scarlet cloth, from two or three
capital traders at, or near, St. Louis, and every
article most saleable with the Indians. Both par-
ties knew each other, and had confidence in each
other; and having this advantage over our band of
adventurers, it does not appear that Mr. Mackenzie,
and Mr. Sublet felt any apprehensions or jealousy

of the new comers from Boston; but treated them
with friendship, and the latter with confidence and
cordiality; the former gentleman being, in a manner, retired from business, except through numerous agents. He owns a small steam-boat called
the Yellow Stone, the name of one of the branches
of the Missouri river. Through such means the
Indians are supplied with all they want; and they
appeared not to wish to have any thing to do with
any one else, especially the adventurous Yankees.
These old established traders enjoy a friendly influence, or prudent command, over those savages,
that seems to operate to the exclusion of every
one else; and this appeared from the manner in
which they treated us, which was void of every
thing like jealousy, or fear of rivalship. Their
policy was to incorporate us with their own troop.

We put our goods, and other baggage on board
the steam-boat Otter, and proceeded two hundred
and sixty miles up the Missouri river, which is as
far as the white people have any settlements. We
were obliged to proceed very slowly and carefully
on account of the numerous *snags* and *sawyers*
with which this river abounds. They are trees
that have been loosened, and washed away from
the soft banks of the river. They are detained
by sand-banks, or by other trees, that have floated
down some time before. Those of them whose
sharp branches point opposite the stream are the
snags, against which boats are often impelled, as
they are not visible above water, and many are
sunk by the wounds these make in their bows.
The *sawyers* are also held fast by their roots, while
the body of the tree whips up and down, alternate-
ly visible and concealed beneath the surface. These

3

are the chief terrors of the Missouri and the Mississippi rivers.   As to crocodiles they are little regarded, being more afraid of man than he of them.
On account of these snags and sawyers, boatmen
avoid passing in the night, and are obliged to keep a
sharp look out in the day-time.   The sawyers when
forced to the bottom or near it by a strong current,
or by eddies, rise again with such force that few
boats can withstand the shock.   The course of the
boat was so tediously slow, that many of us concluded to get out and walk on the banks of the river.
This, while it gave us agreeable exercise, was of
some service in lightening our boat, for with other
passengers from St. Louis, we amounted to a considerable crew.   The ground was level, and free
from underwood.   We passed plenty of deer, wild
turkeys, and some other wild fowl unknown to us,
and expected to find it so all the way.

We arrived at a town or settlement called *Independence.*   This is the last white settlement on
our route to the Oregon, and this circumstance
gave a different cast to our peregrination, and operated not a little on our hopes, and our fears, and
our imaginations.   Some of our company began to
ask each other some serious questions ; such as,
Where are we going? and what are we going for? and
sundry other questions, which would have been wiser
had we asked them before we left Cambridge, and
ruminated well on the answers.   But *Westward
ho!* was our watchword, and checked all doubts,
and silenced all expressions of fear.

Just before we started from this place, a company of sixty-two in number arrived from St. Louis, under the command of *William Sublet, Esq.*,
an experienced Indian trader, bound, like ourselves,

to the American Alps, the Rocky Mountains, and we joined company with him, and it was very lucky that we did. Our minds were not entirely easy. We were about to leave our peaceable countrymen, from whom we had received many attentions and much kindness, to go into a dark region of savages, of whose customs, manners, and language, we were entirely ignorant, — to go we knew not whither, — to encounter we knew not what. We had already sacrificed our amphibious wagons, the result of so much pains and cost. Here two of our company left us, named Kilham and Weeks. Whether they had any real cause of dissatisfaction with our Captain, or whether they only made that an excuse to quit the expedition and return home early, it is not for me to say. I suspect the abandonment of our travelling vehicles cooled their courage. We rested at Independence ten days ; and purchased, by Captain Sublet's advice, two yoke of oxen, and fifteen sheep, as we learnt that we ought not to rely entirely upon transient game from our fire-arms for sustenance, especially as we were now going among a savage people who would regard us with suspicion and dread, and treat us accordingly. From this place we travelled about twenty-five miles a day.

Nothing occurred worth recording, till we arrived at the first Indian settlement, which was about seventy miles from Independence. They appeared to us a harmless people, and not averse to our passing through their country. Their persons were rather under size, and their complexion dark. As they lived near the frontier of the whites, they were not unacquainted with their usages and customs. They have cultivated spots or little farms, on which they raise corn and pumpkins. They generally go out once a year to hunt, accompanied by their women; and on killing the Buffalo, or Bison, what they do not use on the spot, they dry to eat through the winter. To prevent a famine, however, it is their custom to keep a large number of dogs; and they eat them as we do mutton and lamb. This tribe have imitated the white people in having fixed and stationary houses. They stick poles in the ground in a circular form, and cover them with buffalo-skins, and put earth over the whole, leaving at the top an aperture for the smoke, but small enough to be covered with a buffalo-skin in case of rain or snow. — We found here little game; but honey-bees in abundance.

We travelled on about a hundred miles farther, when we came to a large *prairie*, which name the French have given to extensive tracts of land, mostly level, destitute of trees, and covered with tall, coarse grass. They are generally dreary plains, void of water, and rendered more arid by the Indian custom of setting fire to the high grass once or twice a year to start the game that has taken shelter there, which occasions a hard crust unfavorable to any vegetable more substantial than grass. At this unpromising spot, three more of our company took French leave of us, there being, it seems, dissatisfaction on both sides; for each complained of the other. The names of the seceders were Livermore, Bell, and Griswell. In sixteen days more we reached the River *La Platte*, the water of which is foul and muddy. We were nine days passing this dreary *prairie*. We were seven and twenty days winding our way along the borders of the La Platte, which river we could not leave on account of the scarcity of water in the dry and comfortless plains. Here we slaughtered the last of our live stock, and at night we came to that region where buffaloes are often to be found ; but we suffered some sharp gnawings of hunger before we obtained one, and experienced some foretaste of difficulties to come.

The Missouri Territory is a vast wilderness, consisting of immense plains, destitute of wood and of water, except on the edges of streams that are found near the turbid La Platte. This river owes its source to the Rocky mountains, and runs pretty much through the territory, without enlivening or fructifying this desert. Some opinion may be formed of it by saying that for the space of six hundred miles, we may be said to have been deprived of the benefits of two of the elements, *fire* and *water*. Here were, be sure, buffaloes, but after we had killed them we had no wood or vegetables of any kind wherewith to kindle a fire for cooking. We were absolutely compelled to dry the dung of the buffalo as the best article we could procure for cooking our coarse beef. That grumbling, discontent, and dejection should spring up amongst us, was what no one can be surprised at learning. We were at times very miserable, and our commander could be no less so ; but we had put our hands to the plough, and most of us were too stuffy to flinch, and sneak off for home without reaching the Rocky Mountains ; still hunger is hunger, and the young and the strong feel the greatest call for food. Every one who goes to sea may lay his account for coming to short allowance, from violent storms, head winds, damaged vessel, and the like ; but for a band of New-England

3*

men to come to short allowance upon land, with guns, powder, and shot, was a new idea to our Oregon adventurers, who had not prepared for it in the article of hard bread, or flour, or potatoes, or that snug and wholesome article, *salt fish*, so plenty at Marblehead and Cape Ann, and so convenient to carry. When the second company shall march from the seat of science, Cambridge, we would advise them to pack up a few quintals of salt fish, and a few pounds of ground sago, and salep, as a teaspoonful of it mixed with boiling water, will make three pints of good gruel, and also a competent supply of portable soup.

Buffaloes were plenty enough. We saw them in frightful droves, as far as the eye could reach, appearing at a distance as if the ground itself was moving like the sea. Such large armies of them have no fear of man. They will travel over him, and make nothing of him. Our company after killing ten or twelve of them, never enjoyed the benefit of more than two of them, the rest being carried off by the wolves before morning. Beside the scarcity of meat, we suffered for want of good and wholesome water. The La Platte is warm and muddy; and the use of it occasioned a diarrœha in several of our company. Dr. Jacob Wyeth, brother of the Captain, suffered not a little from this cause. — Should the reader wonder how we proceeded so rapidly on our way without stopping to inquire, he must bear in mind that we were still under the guidance of Captain Sublet, who knew every step of the way, and had actually resided four years in different green valleys that are here and there in the Rocky Mountains. To me it seems that we must have perished for want of sustenance in the deserts of Missouri, had we been by ourselves. It may have been good policy in Sublet, to attach us to him. He probably saw our rawness in an adventure so ill provided for as ours actually was.   But for him we should hardly have provided ourselves with live stock; and but for him we should probably never have reached the American Alps. By this time every man began to think for himself.

We travelled six days on the south branch of the La Platte, and then crossed over to the north branch, and on this branch of it, we travelled eighteen days. But the first three days we could not find sufficient articles of food ; and what added to our distress was the sickness of several of our company. We noticed many trails of the savages, but no Indians. The nearer we approached the range of the mountains the thicker were the trees. After travelling twelve days longer we came to the Black Hills. They are so called from their thick growth of cedar. Here is the region of rattle snakes, and the largest and fiercest bears, — a very formidable animal, which it is not prudent for a man to attack alone. I have known some of the best hunters of Sublet's company to fire five an six balls at one before he fell. We were four days in crossing these dismal looking hills. They would be called mountains, were they not in the neighbourhood of the Rocky Mountains, whose peaks overtop every thing, and elevate themselves into the region of everlasting frost and snow. Our sick suffered extremely in ascending these hills, some of them slipped off the horses and mules they rode on, from sheer weakness, brought on by the bowel complaint already mentioned; among these was Dr.

Wyeth, our Captain's brother, who never had a constitution fit to encounter such an expedition. And yet we could not leave them under the care of a man, or two or three men, and pass on without them, to follow us, when they were able. It was to me particularly grievous to think that he, who was to take care of the health of the company, was the first who was disabled from helping himself or others, and this one a blood relation. It required a man of a firmer make than Dr. Jacob Wyeth to go through such a mountainous region as the one we were in : a man seldom does a thing right the first time.

From the North branch we crossed over to what was called Sweet-water Creek. This water being cool, clear, and pleasant, proved a good remedy for our sick, as their bowel complaints were brought on and aggravated by the warm, muddy waters of the Missouri territory we had passed through. We came to a huge rock in the shape of a bowl upside down. It bore the name of Independence, from, it is said, being the resting-place of Lewis and Clarke on the 4th of July ; but according to the printed journal of those meritorious travellers, they had not reached, or entered, the American Alps on the day of that memorable epoch. Whether we are to consider the rock Independence as fairly in the Rocky Mountains, let others determine. We had now certainly begun our ascent to those lofty regions, previous to which we had to pass the chief branch of the river La Platte ; but we had no boat whatever for the purpose ; and had we not been in the company of Captain Sublet, it is hard to say what we should have done short of going a great way round. Here I, and others were entirely convinced that we were engaged in an expedition without being provided with the means to accomplish it. Our boats and wagons we had disposed of at St. Louis, and here we were on the banks of a river without even a canoe. Captain Clarke brought his canoes to the foot of the range of mountains and there left them. The reader will understand that not only the Missouri river, but the Yellow-stone river, the La Platte, and many other smaller ones commence by small beginnings in the Black Hills, and in the Rocky Mountains, and increase in size and depth as they proceed down to join the Arkansa, or the Canadian river, and finally the Mississippi, and so run into the vast salt ocean. Whether it was Captain Sublet's own invention, or an invention of the Indians, we know not, but the contrivance we used is worth mentioning. They called it a *Bull-boat*. They first cut a number of willows (which grow every where near the banks of all the rivers we had travelled by from St. Louis), of about an inch and a half diameter at the butt end, and fixed them in the ground at proper distances from each other, and as they approached nearer one end they brought them nearer together, so as to form something like the bow. The ends of the whole were brought and bound firmly together, like the ribs of a great basket; and then they took other twigs of willow and wove them into those stuck in the ground so as to make a sort of firm, huge basket of twelve or fourteen feet long. After this was completed, they sewed together a number of buffalo-skins, and with them covered the whole; and after the different parts had been trimmed off smooth, a slow fire was made under the Bull-boat, taking care to dry the skins moderately; and as they gradually dried, and acquired a due degree of warmth, they rubbed buffalo-tallow all over the outside of it, so as to allow it to enter into all the seams of the boat, now no longer a willow-basket. As the melted tallow ran down into every seam, hole, and crevice, it cooled into a firm body capable of resisting the water, and bearing a considerable blow without damaging it. Then the willow-ribbed, buffalo-skin, tallowed vehicle was carefully pulled up from the ground, and behold a boat capable of transporting man, horse, and goods over a pretty strong current. At the sight of it, we Yankees all burst out into a loud laugh, whether from surprise, or pleasure, or both, I know not. It certainly was not from ridicule; for we all acknowledged the contrivance would have done credit to *old* New-England.

While Captain Sublet and his company were binding the gunwale of the boat with buffalo-sinews, to give it strength and due hardness, our Captain was by no means idle. He accordingly undertook to make a raft to transport our own goods across the river. Sublet expressed his opinion that it would not answer where the current was strong; but Captain Wyeth is a man not easily to be diverted from any of his notions, or liable to be influenced by the advice of others; so that while Sublet's men were employed on their Bull-boat, Wyeth and a chosen few were making a raft. When finished, we first placed our blacksmith's shop upon it, that is to say, our anvil, and large vice, and other valuable articles belonging to blacksmithery, bar-iron, and steel traps, and alas! a cask of powder, and a number of smaller, but valuable articles. We fixed a rope to our raft, and with some difficulty got

the other end of it across the river to the opposite
bank by a man swimming with a rope in his mouth,
from some distance above the spot he aimed to
reach.   We took a turn of it round a tree.   Captain
Sublet gave it as his opinion that the line would
not be sufficient to command the raft.   But our
Leader was confident that it would ; but when they
had pulled about half way over, the rope broke, and
the raft caught under the limbs of a partly submerged
tree, and tipped it on one side so that we lost our
iron articles, and damaged our goods and a number of
percussion caps.   This was a very serious calamity
and absolutely irreparable.   Almost every disaster
has some benefit growing out of it.   It was even so
here.   Two thirds of our company were sick, and
that without any particular disorder that we can
name, but from fatigue, bad water, scanty food, and
eating flesh half raw.   Add to this, worry of mind,
and serious apprehensions of our fate when the worthy Captain Sublet should leave us ; for he was, under Providence, the instrument of our preservation.
Our own individual sufferings were enough for us to
bear ; but Captain Wyeth had to bear the like, and
more beside, as the responsibility lay heavy upon
him.   Most men would have sunk under it.   At
this point of our journey we were sadly tormen-
ted by musquetoes, that prevented our sleep after
the fatigues of the day.   This little contemptible
insect, which they call here a gnat, disturbed us
more than bears, or wolves, or snakes.

The next day after we started from this unlucky
place, we descried a number of men on horseback,
approaching us at full speed.   Various were our
conjectures.   Captain Sublet had an apprehension
that they might be hostile Indians who fight on

horseback; he therefore ordered every man to make fast his horse as quick as possible, and prepare for battle on foot. But on their near approach, we found them a body of white men called *trappers*, whose occupation is to entrap the beaver and other animals that have valuable furs. Captain Sublet has, for several years, had about two hundred of these trappers in his pay, in and around the Rocky Mountains, and this troop was a party of them. His place of rendezvous for them is at *Pierre's Hole*, by which name they call one of those deep and verdant valleys which are to be found in the Rocky Mountains from the eastern boundary of them to their extreme edge in the west, where the Oregon or Columbia river commences under the name of Clarke's river, some branches of which inosculate with the mighty Missouri on the east. It is to *Pierre's* valley or *Hole*, that his trappers resort to meet their employer every summer. It is here they bring their peltry and receive their pay; and this traffic has been kept up between them a number of years with good faith on both sides, and to mutual satisfaction and encouragement. When Sublet leaves St. Louis, he brings up tobacco, coffee, rice, powder, shot, paint, beads, handkerchiefs and all those articles of finery that please both Indian women and men; and having established that sort of traffic with his friends, the Indians on and in the vicinity of the Rocky Mountains, what chance was there that any small band from Boston, or even Cambridge, could supplant him in the friendship and confidence of his old acquaintance, the Shoshonees, the Black-feet, or any other tribe? He must have seen this at once, and been convinced that nothing like rivalship could

rise up between him and the New-England adventurers. He therefore caressed them, and, in a
manner, incorporated them with his troop.

This gentleman was born in America of French
parents, and partakes largely of those good-humored,
polite, and accommodating manners which distin-
guish the nation he sprang from. The old
French war, and wars on this continent since then,
amply prove how much better Frenchmen concili-
ate the natives than the English. The English and
the Americans, when they come in contact with the
untutored savage, most commonly fight. But not
so the French. They please and flatter the Indian,
give him powder, and balls, and flints, and guns, and
make a Catholic of him, and make out to live in
friendship with the red man and woman of the
wilderness. It is strange that such extremes of
character should meet. Some have said that they
are not so very far distant as others have imagined, –
that the refined French people love war, and the
women paint their faces, grease their hair, and
wear East India blankets, called shawls. — Captain Sublet possesses, doubtless, that conciliating
disposition so characteristic of the French, and
not so frequently found among the English or
Americans; for the decendants of both nations bear
strong marks of the stock they came from. The
French have always had a stronger hold of the
affections of the Indians than any other people.

The trappers kept company with us till we came
to Pierre's-Hole, or valley, which is twelve miles
from the spot where we first met them. Three
or four days after, we were fired on by the Indians
about ten o'clock at night. They had assembled
to about the number of three hundred. They stole

five horses from us, and three from Sublet's company. About the first of July we crossed the highest part or ridge of the mountains. In addition to the mountain composed of earth, sand, and stone, including common rocks, there were certain peaks resembling a loaf of sugar, from a hundred to two hundred feet high ; and some appeared much higher ; I cannot guess their height. They were to us surprising. Their sides deviated but little from perpendicular. They looked at a distance like some light-houses of a conical form, or like our Cambridge glass manufactories ; but how they acquired that form is wonderful. Subsiding waters may have left them so, after washing away sandy materials. But nature is altogether wonderful, in her large works as well as small. How little do we know of the first cause of any thing ! We had to creep round the base of these steep edifices of nature. We now more clearly understand and relish the question of one of our Indians who was carried to England as a show, who, on being shown that elegant pile of stone, the Cathedral of St. Paul, after viewing it in silent admiration, asked his interpreter *whether it was made by men's hands, or whether it grew there.* We might ask the same question respecting these conical mountains. Had the scaffolding of St. Paul's remained, the surprise and wonder of the sensible savage had been less.

It was difficult to keep our feet on these highest parts of the mountains ; some of the pack-horses slipped and rolled over and over, and yet were taken up alive. Those that did not fall were sadly bruised and lamed in their feet and joints. Mules are best calculated, as we experienced, for such difficult travelling. They seem to think, and to judge of the path before them, and will sometimes put their fore feet together and slip down without stepping. They are as sagacious in crossing a river, where there is a current. They will not attempt to go straight over, but will breast the tide by passing obliquely upwards. One of our horses was killed by a fall down one of these precipices, and it was surprising that more of them did not share the like fate. Buffaloes were so scarce here, that we were obliged to feed on our dried meat, and this scarcity continued till after we had gained the head sources of the Columbia river. For the last five days we have had to travel on the Colorado of the West, which is a very long river, and empties into the gulph of California.

On the 4th of July, 1832, we arrived at Lewis's fork, one of the largest rivers in these rocky mountains. It took us all day to cross it. It is half a mile wide, deep, and rapid. The way we managed was this ; one man unloaded his horse, and swam across with him, leading two loaded ones, and unloading the two, brought them back, for two more, and as Sublet's company and our own made over a hundred and fifty, we were all day in passing the river. In returning, my mule, by treading on a round stone, stumbled and threw me off, and the current was so strong, that a bush which I caught hold of only saved me from drowning.

This being Independence-Day, we drank the health of our friends in Massachusetts, in good clear water, as that was the only liquor we had to drink in remembrance of our homes and dear connexions. If I may judge by my own feelings and by the looks of my companions, there was more of melancholy than joy amongst us. We were almost four thousand miles from Boston, and in saying Boston we mean, at the same time our native spot Cambridge, as they are separated by a wooden bridge only. From the north fork of Lewis's river we passed on to an eminence called Teton mountain, where we spent the night. The next day was pleasant, and serene. Captain Sublet came in the evening to enquire how many of our company were sick, as they must ride, it being impossible for them to go on foot any farther. His kindness and attention I never can forget. Dr. Jacob Wyeth, the Captain's brother, George More, and Stephen Burdit were too weak to walk. To accommodate them with horses, Captain Wyeth was obliged to dig a hole in the earth, and therein bury the goods which had been hitherto carried on horseback. In the language of the Trappers this hiding of goods was called *cacher* or hidden treasure, being the French term for 'to hide.' When they dig these hiding-holes they carefully carry the earth on a buffalo-skin to a distance, so as to leave no marks or traces of the ground being dug up or disturbed: and this was done to secure the *cache* from being stolen by the Indians or the whitemen. The goods so hidden are wrapt up in buffalo-skins to keep them dry, before the earth is put over them. Nor is this all; they make a fire over the spot, and all this to prevent the Indians from suspecting that treasure is *caché*, or hidden there, while the owner of it takes care to mark the bearing of the spot on some tree, or rock, or some other object that may lead him to recognise the place again. But I have my doubts whether they who hid the goods will ever return that way to dig up their hidden treasure. We did not meddle with it on our return with Captain Sublet.

On the 5th of July we started afresh rather low-spirited. We looked with sadness on the way before us. The mountain was here pretty thickly timbered down its slopes, and wherever the ground is level. The pines and hemlock trees were generally about eighteen inches through. It had snowed, and we were now at a height where the snow commonly lies all the year round. Which ever way we looked, the region presented a dreary aspect. No one could wonder that even some of us who were in health, were, at times, somewhat home-sick. If this was the case with us, what must have been the feelings of our three sick fellow travellers. We passed through a snow bank three feet deep. We well ones passed on with Captain Sublet to the top of the mountain, and there waited until our sick men came up with us. George Môre fell from his horse through weakness. He might have maintained his seat on level ground, but ascending and descending required more exertion than he could call forth ; and this was the case also with Dr. Wyeth. Burdit made out a little better. When we encamped at night, we endured a snow storm. Sublet's company encamped about two miles from us ; for at best we could hardly keep up with his veteran company. They were old and experienced trappers, and we, compared with them, young and inexperienced soldiers, little imagining that we should ever have to encounter such hardships, in realizing our dreams of making a fortune. Ignorance of the future is not always to be considered among the calamities of man.

Captain Sublet's grand rendezvous, or Head Quarters, was about twelve miles from our encampment. He had there about two hundred trappers, or beaver-hunters; or more properly speaking, *skinners* of entrapped animals; or *peltry-* hunters, for they chased but few of the captured beasts. To these were added about five hundred Indians, of the rank of warriors, all engaged in the same pursuit and traffic of the fur-trade. They were principally the *Flat-heads*, so called from their flattening the heads of their young children, by forcing them to wear a piece of wood, like a bit of board, so as to cause the skull to grow flat, which they consider a mark of beauty even among the females. They are otherwise dandies and belles in their dress and ornaments. This large body of horse made a fine appearance, especially their long hair; for, as there was a pleasant breeze of wind, their hair blew out straight all in one direction, which had the appearance of so many black streamers. When we met they halted and fired three rounds by way of salute, which we returned; and then followed such friendly greetings as were natural and proper between such high contracting powers and great and good allies. This parade was doubtless made by Sublet for the sake of effect. It was showing us, Yankee barbarians, *their Elephants*; — like General and Lord Howe's military display to our commissioners of Congress, on Staten Island, when the British Brothers proposed that celebrated interview; and when Dr. Franklin, Mr. Adams, and some others of the deputation, whose names I do not now recollect, assumed all that careless indifference, very common with the Indians on meeting a white embassy; for the express purpose of conveying an idea, that we, though the weakest in discipline and numbers, are not awe-struck by your fine dress, glittering arms, and full-fed persons.

It was now the 6th of July, 1832, being sixty-four days since we left the settlements of the white people. Captain Sublet encamped his forces; and then pointed out to Captain Wyeth the ground which he thought would be most proper for us; and altogether we looked like a little army. Not but what we felt small compared with our great and powerful allies.

We were overjoyed to think that we had got to a resting-place, where we could repose our weary limbs, and recruit the lost strength of our sick. While Sublet was finishing his business with his Indian trappers, they delivering their peltry, and he remunerating them in his way with cloth, powder, ball, beads, knives, handkerchiefs, and all that gawdy trumpery which Indians admire, together with coffee, rice, and corn, also leather, and other articles, — we, being idle, had time to think, to·reflect, and to be uneasy. We had been dissatisfied for some time, but we had not leisure to communicate it and systematize our grievances. I, with others, had spoken with Captain Sublet, and him we found conversable and communicative. Myself and some others requested Captain Wyeth to call a meeting of his followers, to ask information, and to know what we were now to expect, seeing we had passed over as we supposed the greatest difficulties, and were now nearly four thousand miles from the *Atlantic*, and within four hundred miles of the *Pacific Ocean*, the end and aim of our laborious expedition, the field where we expected to reap our promised harvest. We wished to have what we had been used to at home, — a town meeting, — or a parish meeting, where every freeman has an equal right to speak his sentiments, and to vote there-

on. But Captain Wyeth was by no means inclined
to this democratical procedure. The most he
seemed inclined to, was a *caucus* with a select few ;
of whom neither his own brother, though older
than himself, nor myself, was to be of the number.
After considerable altercation, he concluded to call
a meeting of the whole, on business interesting and
applicable to all. We accordingly met, Captain
Wyeth in the chair, or on the stump, I forget which.
Instead of every man speaking his own mind,
or asking such questions as related to matters that
lay heaviest on his mind, the Captain commenced
the business by ordering the roll to be called ; and
as the names were called, the clerk asked the person if he would go on. The first name was
Nathaniel J. Wyeth, whom we had dubbed *Captain*, who answered — "I shall go on." — The
next was William Nud, who, before he answered,
wished to know what the Captain's plan and intentions were, whether to try to commence a small
colony, or to trap and trade for beaver ? To
which Captain Wyeth replied, that *that* was none
of our business. Then Mr. Nud said, " I shall not
go on ; " and as the names of the rest were called,
there appeared *seven* persons out of the *twenty-one*,
who were determined to return home. Of the
number so determined was, beside myself, Dr. Jacob Wyeth, the Captain's brother, whose strength
had never been equal to such a journey. His constitution forbade it. He was brought up at College.
Here were discontents on both sides ; criminations
and recriminations. A commander of a band of
associated adventurers has a very hard task. The
commanded, whether in a school, or in a regiment,
or company, naturally combine in feeling against

their leader ; and this is so natural that armies are obliged to make very strict rules, and to pursue rigid discipline. It is so also on ship-board. Our merchant ships cannot sail in safety without exacting prompt obedience; and disobedience in the common seamen is mutiny, and mutiny is a high crime, and approximates to piracy. It is pretty much so in these long and distant exploring expeditions. The Captain cannot always with safety satisfy all the questions put to him by those under his command; and it would lead to great inconvenience to entrust any, even a brother, with any information concealed from the rest. There must be secrecy, and there must be confidence. We had travelled through a dreary wilderness, an infinitely worse country than Palestine; yet Moses himself could not have kept together the Israelites without the aid of miracles; and the history we have given of our boat-like arks, and the wreck of our raft, and the loss of our heaviest articles may lead most readers to suspect that our Leader to his Land of Promise was not an inspired man. In saying this, we censure no one, we only lament our common frailty. Reflect a moment, considerate reader! on our humble means, for an expedition of FOUR THOUSAND *miles*, compared with the ample means, rich and complete out-fit, letters of credit, and every thing deemed needful, given to *Captains Lewis* and *Clarke*, under the orders of the government of the United States; and yet they several times came very near starving for the want of food, and of *fuel*, even in the *Oregon* territory! In all books of voyages and travels, who ever heard of the utmost distress for want of wood, leaves, roots, coal, or turf to cook

with? Yet all through the dreary wilderness of
Missouri, we were obliged to use the dung of buffaloes, or eat raw flesh. The reader will scarcely
believe that this was the case even at the mouth
of the Oregon river. Clarke and Lewis had to
buy wood of the Indians, who had hardly enough
for themselves. To be deprived of solid food soon
ends in death; but we were often deprived of the
two elements out of four, *fire* and *water*, and when
on the Rocky mountains, of a *third*, I mean *earth*;
for every thing beneath our feet and around us was
stone. We had, be sure, *air* enough, and too much
too, sometimes enough almost to blow our hair off.

But to return to our dismal list of grievances.
Almost every one of the company wished to go
no farther; but they found themselves too feeble and
exhausted to think of encountering the risk of a
march on foot of three thousand five hundred miles
through such a country as we came. We asked Captain Wyeth to let us have our muskets and a sufficiency of ammunition, which request he refused. Afterwards, he collected all the guns, and after selecting
such as he and his companions preferred, he gave us
the refuse; many of which were unfit for use. There
were two tents belonging to the company, of which
he gave us one; which we pitched about a quarter of
a mile fom his. George More expressed his deter-
mination of returning home, and asked for a horse,
which after considerable difficulty he obtained.
This was July 10th. The Captain likewise supplied his brother with a horse and a hundred dollars.

On the 12th of July, Captain Wyeth, after moving his tent half a mile farther from ours, put himself under the command of Mr. Milton Sublet,

brother of Captain William Sublet so often mentioned. This Captain Milton Sublet had about twenty men under his command, all trappers ; so that hereafter as far as I know, it was Wyeth, Sublet and Co.; so that the reader will understand, that Dr. Jacob Wyeth, Palmer, Law, Batch, and myself concluded to retrace our steps to St. Louis in company with Captain William Sublet, while Captain Nathaniel J. Wyeth remained with Milton Sublet, and his twenty men. I have been unreasonably blamed for leaving my kinsman beyond the Rocky Mountains with only eleven of his company, and that too when we were within about four hundred miles of the mouth of the Columbia, *alias* Oregon river, where it pours into the *boisterous* Pacific Ocean, for such Lewis and Clarke found it to their cost.

The spot where we now were, is a valley, between two mountains, about ten miles wide, so lofty that their tops are covered with snow, while it was warm and pleasant where we pitched our tent. This agreeable valley is called by the trappers *Pierre's-Hole*, as if it were a dismal residence ; and was the most western point that I visited, being about, we conjectured, four hundred miles short of the mouth of the Oregon river, whence the territory derives its name, which Mr. Hall J. Kelly has described as another paradise ! O ! the magic of sounds and inflated words ! Whether Captain Wyeth's expedition was wise or imprudent we are not prepared to say ; but under existing circumstances, half of his company having left him, and among them his own brother, the surgeon of the expedition, we cannot see what better he could have done than to ally himself to an experienced band of hunters, as a step necessary to his own preservation. He was three thousand and five hundred miles from the Atlantic Ocean, with only eleven men, and half his goods lost or expended, and no resource of supply short of St. Louis, nineteen hundred miles from them. Had not the Sublets been with them from that place through the wilderness of Missouri and La Platte, it is hardly probable they would have ever reached the west side of the Rocky Mountains. In passing judgment on this strange expedition, we must take in, beside facts, probabilities and casualties.

On the 17th of July, Captain Wyeth and Captain Milton Sublet set out westward with their respective men to go to Salmon river to winter. The former had eleven beside himself: that river they computed at two hundred miles distance. Wyeth accordingly purchased twenty-five horses from the Indians, who had a great number, and those very fine, and high-spirited. Indeed the Western region seems the native and congenial country for horses. They were, however, delayed till the next day. But when they were about moving, they perceived a drove of something, whether buffaloes or men they could not determine with the naked eye; but when aided by the glass, they recognised them for a body of the *Black-foot* tribe of Indians, a powerful and warlike nation. As this movement was evidently hostile, Captain Milton Sublet dispatched two men to call on his brother, who was about eight miles off, for assistance; when Captain William Sublet ordered every man to get ready immediately. We had about five hundred friendly Indian warriors with us, who expressed their willingness to join in our defence.

As soon as we left Captain Wyeth we joined Captain Sublet, as he said that no white man should be there unless he was to be under his command; and his reason for it was that in case they had to fight the Indians, no one should flinch or sneak out of the battle. It seems that when the Black-foot Indians saw us moving in battle array, they appeared to hesitate; and at length they displayed a white flag as an ensign of peace; but Sublet knew their treacherous character. The chief of the friendly Flat-heads and Antoine rode together, and concerted this savage arrangement; to ride up and accost them in a friendly manner; and when the Black-foot chief should take hold of the Flat-head chief's hand in token of friendship, then the other was to shoot him, which was instantly done! and at that moment the Flat-head chief pulled off the Black-foot's scarlet robe, and returned with the Captain to our party unhurt. As soon as the Black-foot Indians recovered from their surprise, they displayed a *red* flag, and the battle began. This was *Joab* with a vengeance, — *Art thou in health my brother?*

The Black-foot chief was a man of consequence in his nation. He not only wore on this occasion a robe of scarlet cloth, probably obtained from a Christian source, but was decorated with beads valued there at sixty dollars. The battle commenced on the Prairie. As soon as the firing began on both sides, the squaws belonging to the Black-foot forces, retreated about fifty yards into a small thicket of wood, and there threw up a ridge of earth by way of entrenchment, having first piled up a number of logs cob-fashion, to which the men at length fell back, and from

5

which they fired upon us, while some of their party with the women were occupied in deepening the trench. Shallow as it was, it afforded a considerable security to an Indian, who will often shoot a man from behind a tree near to its root, while the white man is looking to see his head pop out at man's height. This has taught the United States troops, to load their muskets while lying on their backs, and firing in an almost supine posture. When the Duke of Saxe-Weimar was in Cambridge, he noticed this, to him, novel mode of firing, which he had never before seen; and this was in a volunteer company of militia. — I do not mean to say that the Indians fired only in a supine posture; when they had loaded they most commonly rose up and fired, and then down on the ground again to re-load. — In this action with the formidable Blackfoot tribe, Captain Nathaniel J. Wyeth's party had no concern. He himself was in it a very short time, but retired from the contest doubtless for good reasons. After contesting the matter with the warlike tribe about six hours, Captain Sublet found it of little avail to fight them in this way. He therefore determined to charge them at once, which was accordingly done. He led, and ordered his men to follow him, and this proved effectual. Six beside himself first met the savages hand to hand; of these seven, four were wounded, and one killed. The Captain was wounded in his arm and shoulder-blade. The Indians did not, however, retreat entirely, so that we kept up a random fire until dark; the ball and the arrows were striking the trees after we could see the effects of one and of the other. There was something terrific to our men in their arrows. The idea of a barbed arrow stick-

ing in a man's body, as we had observed it in the
deer and other animals, was appaling to us all, and
it is no wonder that some of our men recoiled at
it.   They regarded a leaden bullet much less.   We
may judge from this the terror of the savages on
being met the first time by fire arms, — a sort of
thunder and lightning followed by death without
seeing the fatal shot.

In this battle with the Indians, not one of those
who had belonged to Captain Wyeth's company
received any injury.   There were, however, seven
white men of Sublet's company killed, and thirteen
wounded.   Twenty-five of our Indians were killed,
and thirty-five wounded.   The next morning a
number of us went back to the Indian fort, so
called, where we found one dead man and two
women, and also twenty-five dead horses, a proof
that the Black-foot were brave men.   The number
of them was uncertain.   We calculated that they
amounted to about three hundred.   We guessed
that the reason the three dead bodies were left at
the entrenchment was, that they had not enough left
to carry off their dead and wounded.   This affair
delayed Captain Wyeth ·three days, and Captain
Sublet ten days.   The names of those who left
Captain Wyeth to return home, were Dr. Jacob
Wyeth, John B. Wyeth, his cousin, William Nud,
Theophilus Beach, R. L. Wakefield, Hamilton
Law, George More, —— Lane, and Walter Palmer.
The names of those who remained attached to
Captain Wyeth, and who went on with him to
Salmon river, are J. Woodman Smith, G. Sargent,
—— Abbot, W. Breck, S. Burditt, —— Ball, St.
Clair, C. Tibbits, G. Trumbull, and —— Whittier.
When they had gone three days journey from us,

as they were riding securely in the middle of the afternoon, about thirty of the Black-foot Indians, who lay in ambush about twenty yards from them, suddenly sprang up and fired. The surprise occasioned the horses to wheel about, which threw off George More, and mortally wounded one of the men, Alfred K. Stevens. As the Indians knew that More could not get away from them, they passed him, and about twenty Indians were coming up the hill where they were. Eight or ten Indians followed up while only five trappers had gained the hill. They were considering how to save George More, when one of them shot him through the head, which was a better fate than if they had taken him alive, as they would have tortured him to death.

We have said that Captain Wyeth and the few who had concluded to go on with him, were ready to begin their march for Salmon river. On this occasion Captain Milton Sublet escorted them about one hundred miles, so as to protect them from the enraged Black-feet, and then left them to take care of themselves for the winter; and this is the last tidings we have had of Captain Nathaniel J. Wyeth, and his reduced band of adventurers. If we have been rightly informed, their chief hope was residing on a pleasant river where there was plenty of salmon, and probably elk and deer, and water-fowl; and we hope fuel, for to our surprise, we learnt that wood for firing was among their great wants. I have since been well-informed that in the valley of Oregon, so much extolled for its fertility and pleasantness, wood to cook with is one among their scarcest and very dear articles of necessity. From all accounts, except those given to the public by Mr. Kelly, there is not a district at the mouth of any large river more unproductive than that of the *Columbia*, and it seems that this is pretty much the case from the tide water of that river to where it empties into the ocean.

The Flat-head Indians are a brave and we had reason to believe a sincere people. We had many instances of their honesty and humanity. They do not lie, steal, nor rob any one, unless when driven too near to starvation ; and then any man black, white, or red will seize any thing to save himself from an agonizing death. The Flat-heads were well dressed. They wore buck-skin frocks and pantaloons, and moccasins, with seldom any thing on their heads. They draw a piece of fresh buffalo hide on their feet, and at night sleep with their feet not far from the fire, and in the morning find their shoes sitting as snug to their feet as if they had been measured by the first shoe-maker in Boston. It is probable that no people have so little shoe-pinching as these savages. I never heard any one complain of corns, or kibed-heels, severe as the weather is in winter. The women wear moccasins also, but whether made in the same extempore method as those of the men, I know not. I suspect they must experience some shoe-pinching. They wear a petticoat, and a frock of some sort of leather, according to fancy, but all decent and comfortable. In rainy weather, or when very cold, they throw a buffalo-skin over their shoulders, with the fur inside. They have no stationary wigwams ; but have a sort of tent, which they fix down or remove with facility. In Major Long's book may be seen an engraved representation of them. Their mode of cooking is by roasting and boiling. They

5*

will pick a goose, or a brant, and run a stick through its body and so roast it, without taking out its entrails.   They are, according to our notions, very nasty cooks.

I know not what to say of their religion.   I saw nothing like images, or any objects of worship whatever, and yet they appeared to keep a sabbath; for there is a day on which they do not hunt nor gamble, but sit moping all day and look like fools. There certainly appeared among them an honor, or conscience, and sense of justice.   They would do what they promised, and return our strayed horses, and lost articles.   Now and then, but rarely, we found a pilferer, but not oftener than among the frontier white people.   The Indians of all tribes are disposed to give you something to eat.   It is a fact that we never found an Indian of any tribe disposed to treat us with that degree of inhospitality that we experienced in crossing the Alleghany Mountains, in the State of Pennsylvania.

The Black-foot tribe are the tallest and stoutest men of any we have seen, nearly or quite six feet in stature, and of a lighter complexion than the rest.

The Indian warriors carry muskets, bows, and arrows, the last in a quiver.   The bows are made of walnut, about three feet long, and the string of the sinews of the buffalo, all calculated for great elasticity, and will reach an object at a surprising distance.   It was to us a much more terrific weapon of war than a musket.   We had one man wounded in the thigh by an arrow; he was obliged to ford a river in his hasty retreat, and probably took a chill, which occasioned a mortification, of which he died. The arrows are headed with flint as sharp as broken glass; the other end of the arrow is furnished with an eagle's feather to steady its flight. Some of these aboriginals, as we learn from Lewis, Clarke, and Major Long, especially the last, have shields or targets; some so long as to reach from the head to the ancle. Now the question is how came our North American Indians with bows and arrows? It is not likely that they invented them, seeing they so exactly resemble the bows and arrows of the old world, the Greeks and Romans. They are the same weapon to a feather. This is a fresh proof that our savage tribes of this continent emigrated from the old one; and I have learned from a friend to whom I am indebted for several ideas, which no one could suppose to have originated with myself, that the Indian's bow goes a great way to settle a disputed point respecting what part of the old world the ancestors of our Indians came from, — whether Asia or Europe. Now the Asiatic bow and our Indian bow are of a different form. The first has a straight piece in the middle, like the cross-bow, being such an one as is commonly depicted in the hands of Cupid; whereas our Indian bow is a section of a circle, while the Persian or Asiatic bow has two wings extending from a straight piece in the middle. Hence we have reason to conclude that the first comers from the old world to the new, came not from those regions renowned for their cultivation of the arts and sciences. The idea that our North American Indians came over from Scythia, that is, the northern part, so called, of Europe and Asia, whether it is correct to call them Scythians, Tartars, or Russians, I leave others to determine. We

have many evidences that our Northern Indians
have a striking resemblance in countenance, color,
and person to the most northern tribes of Tartars,
who inhabit Siberia, or Asiatic Russia.   The Black-
foot Indians who inhabit small rivers that empty
into the Missouri, resemble in mode of living, manners, and character, the Calmuc Tartars.   Both
fight on horse-back, both are very brave, and both
inured to what we should consider a very hard life
as it regards food.   Both avoid as much as they
can stationary dwellings, and use tents made with
skins.

On this subject we ought not to omit mentioning
that the Indians on all sides of the Rocky mountains have several customs both among the men
and the *women*, which might lead some to conclude
that our Northern and Western Indians descended
from the Israelites ; and this similarity is certainly
very remarkable ; yet there is one very strong fact
against that hypothesis, namely, there is not the
least trace amongst our Indians of the *eight-day
rite* of the Jewish males, which sore, and, to us,
strange ceremony would hardly have been forgotten,
had it been practised by our Indians.   If our idea
be well-founded on this subject, the custom could
have originated only in warm and redundant climates, so that had Moses marched first from the
shores of the Baltic, as did the Goths, instead of the
shores of the Red-sea, the Jews never would have
been subjected to the operation of circumcision.

After all, it is very likely that the Persians came
from a different stock from that which peopled the
Western and Northern parts of America,— I mean
from the warmer regions of Asia.   They seem possessed of more delicate marks of person and of mind

than the fighting savages of the North. There appears to be a strong line of separation between them, as far as our information goes.

To return to our own story. After the battle at Pierre's Valley, I had an opportunity of seeing a specimen of Indian surgery in treating a wound. An Indian squaw first sucked the wound perfectly dry, so that it appeared white as chalk; and then she bound it up with a piece of dry buck-skin as soft as woollen cloth, and by this treatment the wound began to heal, and soon closed up, and the part became sound again. The sucking of it so effectually may have been from an apprehension of a poisoned arrow. But who taught the savage Indian that a person may take poison into his mouth without any risk, as the poison of a rattle-snake without harm, provided there be no scratch or wound in the mouth, so as to admit it into the blood?

Three of the men that left Captain Wyeth when I did, enlisted with Captain Sublet to follow the trapping business for the period of one year, namely, Wakefield, Nud, and Lane, leaving Dr. Jacob Wyeth, H. Law, T. Beach, W. Palmer, and myself. We accordingly set out on the twenty-eighth day of July, 1832, with Captain William Sublet, for home; and thus ended all my fine prospects and flattering expectations of acquiring fortune, independence, and ease, and all my hopes that the time had now come in the order of Providence, when that uncultivated tract, denominated the *Oregon Territory*, was to be changed into a fruitful field, and the haunt of savages and wild beasts made the happy abode of refined and dignified man. — Mr. Hall J. Kelly published about two

years since a most inflated and extravagant account
of that western tract which extends from the Rocky
Mountains to the shore of the Pacific Ocean. He
says of it that no portion of the globe presents a
more fruitful soil, or a milder climate, or equal
facilities for carrying into effect the great purposes
of a free and enlightened nation; — that a country
so full of those natural means which best contrib-
ute to the comforts and conveniences of life, is
worthy the occupancy of a people disposed to support a free representative government, and to establish civil, scientific, and religious institutions. —
and all this and much more to the same effect after
Lewis and Clarke's history of their expedition
had been published, and very generally read; yet
this extravagant and fallacious account of the Oregon was read and believed by some people not destitute of a general information of things, nor unused
to reading; but there were circles of people, chiefly among young farmers and journeymen mechanics, who were so thoroughly imbued with these
extravagant notions of making a fortune by only
going over land to the other side of the globe, to
the Pacific Ocean, that a person who expressed a
doubt of it was in danger of being either affronted,
or, at least, accused of being moved by envious feelings. After a score of people had been enlisted in
this Oregon expedition, they met together to feed
and to magnify each other's hopes and visionary notions, which were wrought up to a high degree of
extravagance, so that it was hardly safe to advise
or give an opionion adverse to the scheme. When
young people are so affected, it is in vain to reason
with them; and when such sanguine persons are
determined to fight, or to marry, it is dangerous to

attempt to part them ; and when they have their own way and get their belly full of fight, and of matrimony, there comes a time of cool reflection. The first stage of our reflection began at St. Louis, when we parted with our amphibious wagons, in which we all more or less took a pride. Every one there praised the ingenuity of the contrivance and construction of them for roads and rivers such as at Cambridge, and other places near to Boston ; but we were assured at St. Louis, that they were by no means calculated for our far distant journey. We were reminded that Lewis and Clarke carried canoes almost to the foot of the Rocky Mountains, by the route of Missouri river, but were obliged to leave them there, and ascend mountains so very steep, that sometimes their loaded horses slipped and rolled over and over, down into lower ground sixty or seventy feet. This may serve to show, among other things, how ill-informed Captain Wyeth and his company were of the true condition of the country through which they had to pass. We expected to support ourselves with game by our fire-arms, and therefore powder and shot were the articles we took the most care to be provided with. Nor were we followers undeceived before we were informed at St. Louis, that it would be necessary to take oxen and sheep to be slaughtered on the route for our support. We also found it advisable to sell at that place the large number of axes, great and small, with which we had encumbered our wagons. All these occurrences, following close after one another, operated to damp our ardor ; and it was this probably that operated so powerfully on W. Bell, Livermore, and Griswold, that they *cut* and run away before we entered upon the difficulties and hardships of our expedition.

Nothing of importance occurred for the first ten days after we left Pierre's Valley. Our huntsmen were abroad in pursuit of buffaloes, when they were alarmed at the sight of a large body of the Black-foot tribe who had been watching our movements. Captain Sublet was not a little alarmed, for he had with him his whole stock of furs, very large in quantity and valuable in quality, which we were told would be worth eighty thousand dollars in St. Louis. But all the world exaggerates ; nor even were we of the Oregon expedition entirely free from it, although not to be compared with Hall Jackson Kelly, who never stops short of superlatives, if we may judge by his publications. But he says, by way of apology, that it is needful that the friends of the contemplated Oregon colony should possess a little of the active and vital principle of enthusiasm, that shields against disappointments, and against the presumptuous opinions and insults of others. Now the fact is, the sanguine and enthusiastic Mr. Kelly was never in that country, nor nearer to it than Boston ; and his zeal in the colonization of that dreary territory led him to believe what he wished, and to disbelieve every thing adverse to his favorite enterprise. He had a right to enjoy his opinion ; but when he took unwearied pains to make ignorant people believe as he did, he was the remote cause of much misery and lasting regret in more than half the adventurers from Cambridge. If the blind lead the blind, we know what will be the consequence. But our business is not to censure from a disposition to find fault, but to warn others from falling into the errors and difficulties which attended me and my companions, and chiefly through the misinformation of persons who never saw the country.

Each man, when we left St. Louis, was allowed to carry but ten pounds' weight of his own private baggage, and not every one to encumber his march with whatever he chose; and we adhered to that order on our return. We were ten days in passing over the Rocky Mountains in going, and nine in returning; and I repeat it as my fixed opinion, that we never should have reached the western foot of the mountains had we not been under the guard and guidance of Captain Sublet, and his experienced company. He was acquainted with the best way, and the best mode of travelling. He knew the Indian chiefs and they knew him, and each confided in the other. An anecdote will illustrate this. There was a hunters' fort or temporary place of defence occupied by about a dozen white beaver-trappers from St. Louis, where were deposited furs, and goods belonging to the troop of trappers, and that to a considerable amount. One day this small garrison was alarmed at the sight of about six hundred warriors approaching on horseback. Upon this they barred their gate, and closed every door and window against the Indians, but with faint hopes of repelling such a powerful host of well-armed savages; for they had no other idea but that they had come for their destruction. But when the Indians saw them shutting themselves up, they displayed the white flag, and made signs to the white men to open their fort, for they came to trade and not to fight. And the little garrison thought it better to trust to Indian honor

6

than risk savage slaughter or captivity; and accordingly they unbarred their doors and let the chiefs in with every expression of cordiality and confidence.   After remaining nine days, they departed in peace.   And what ought to be recorded to their honor, the white people did not miss a single article, although axes, and utensils, and many other things were lying about, desirable to Indians.   The savages did not consider, as white men too often do, — that "*might is right.*"   When I expressed my surprise at it, one of the white trappers replied, " Why, the word of these trading Indians is *as good as the Bible.*"

We were surprised to find the Indians in the vicinity of the mountains, and all round Pierre's Valley, and the Black-foot tribe, and the Shoshonees, or Snake-tribe, so well provided with muskets, powder and ball, woollen cloth, and many other articles, until we were informed that Mr. Mackenzie, an established and wealthy Indian trader, had long supplied them with every article they desired.   Had the Captain of our band been acquainted with this fact, and also been informed of the trading connexion between the Indians and the two brothers, William and Milton Sublet, before he started from home, we should have avoided a great deal of trouble, and he escaped a great deal of expense, and for aught I know, suffering; for the last we heard of him, he was to pass the winter at the Salmon river.

From all I could learn, St. Louis was the depot, or head-quarters of the commerce with the Indians. Mackenzie, I was informed, has a steam-boat called the Yellow-stone, by which he keeps up a trade with the natives inhabiting the region watered by

the river of that name.   The *Yellow-stone* is a noble
river, being eight hundred and thirty-seven miles
from the point where Captain Clarke reached it
to the Missouri, and is so far navigable for batteaux;
and eight hundred and fifty feet wide at its conflu-
ence with the river just named.   By all accounts,
the superiority of the Yellow-stone river over the
Columbia, or Oregon, for a settlement of New-
England adventurers, in point of fertility, climate,
and pleasantness, is such as to impress one with
regret that ever we extended our views beyond it;
for the lamentable fact is, that the trade with the
Indians all round the Rocky Mountains, and beyond
it to the Oregon territory and Columbia river, is
actually forestalled, or pre-occupied by wealthy,
established, and experienced traders residing at, or
near St. Louis, while we are more than twelve
hundred miles in their rear, and very far behind
them in time.   Beside all these considerations, we
may add another of great importance; I mean the
fact, that Mackenzie's and Sublet's white trappers,
or hunters, are a sort of half Indians in their manners
and habits, and could assimilate with them, while we
are strangers to the savages, and they to us, with all
the dislikes natural to both sides.   Captain Sublet,
who appears to be a worthy character, and of sound
judgment, perceived this, and must have seen, at
once, that he had nothing to fear from us, and
therefore he paid us great attention, conciliated and
made use of us, and while he aided us, he benefit-
ted his own concern, and all without the least spice
of jealousy, well knowing the impossibility, under
existing circumstances, that we could supplant him
in the affections of the red men of Missouri and
Oregon.

The white traders, and the Indians have, if we may so term it, an annual *Fair*, that has been found by experience profitable to both sides. It is true the white trader barters a tawdry bauble of a few cents' value, for a skin worth fifty of it. And so have we in our India shawls, and, a few years since, in Leghorn hats, in which we were taxed as high as the white merchant taxes the equally silly Indian. Coffee was sold at two dollars a pound, and so was tobacco. Indeed some of us gave that price to Mr. Nathaniel J. Wyeth for the latter article, a luxury more coveted by men in our situation, anxious and fatigued as we were, than whisky or brandy. This was the case under Lewis and Clarke. When deprived of tobacco, they cut up the old handles of tomahawks, which had been used as pipes, and chewed the wood for the sake of its smell and smack. It is not a singular case. It has been experienced among sailors at sea. They have pined more for the lulling effects of that nauseous weed than for ardent spirits; and it has been known that men will mutiny sooner when deprived of their tobacco, than when deprived of their usual food and rum. There was no small grumbling on being obliged to buy tobacco out of what we thought common stock, at the rate above mentioned, being, as we thought, all members of a commonwealth.

The following may serve to show the knowledge or instinct of horses.

When marching on our return home in the troop of Captain Sublet, not far from the eastern declivity of the Rocky Mountains, we were met by a large body of Indians on horseback. Sublet generally kept seven videts about two miles ahead of his main body. The horses of this advanced guard suddenly refused to go on, and turned round, and appeared alarmed, but the riders knew not the cause of it. Captain Sublet rode up, and said, that he knew by the behaviour of the horses that there was an enemy ahead. He said there was a valley several miles off where he apprehended we might be attacked. He therefore ordered every man to examine his arms, and be ready for action. After riding a few miles we discovered a large moving body of a living something. Some of us thought it was a drove of buffaloes; but the Captain said no, because they were of different colors, whereas bisons, or buffaloes appear all of one color. After viewing them through his glass, he said they were a body of the Black-foot tribe, who had on their war dresses, with their faces painted, bare heads, and other signs of hostility.

Their appearance was very singular, and, to some of us, terrible. There was a pretty fresh breeze of wind, so as to blow the long manes and tales of their horses out straight. Nor was this all: the wind had the same effect on the long black hair of the warriors, which gave them not only a grotesque but a terrific appearance. Added to all this, they kept up a most horrid yell or war-hoop. They rode up and completely surrounded us; and then all was silent. Captain Sublet rode up to the chief, and expressed his hope that all was peace. The savage replied that there should be peace on their part, on condition that Sublet should give them *twenty-five pounds of tobacco*, which was soon complied with, when the Indian army remounted their horses, and rode off at full speed as they came on: and we

6*

pushed off with like speed, lest they should repent their bargain and return upon us to mend it.

Who will say that this gallant body of cavalry were not wiser than the common run of white soldiers, to make peace for a *quid?* and thereby save their horses and their own skins? Out of what book did this corps of savage dragoons learn that discretion was the better part of valor? — We answer, From out of that book of Nature which taught the videts' horses that an enemy was in the wind. The horse is the dumbest of all beasts. He is silent under torture. He never groans but once, and that is his *last.* Did they roar like bulls, or squeal like hogs, they would be useless in an army. That noble animal suffers from man a shameful weight of cruel usage in town and country.

The wild horses are a great curiosity. They traverse the country, and stroll about in droves from a dozen to twenty or thirty; and always appear to have a leader, like a gander to a flock of geese. When our own horses were feeding fettered around our encampments, the wild horses would come down to them, and seem to examine them, as if counting them; and would sometimes come quite up to them if we kept out of sight; but when they discovered us, they would one and all give a jump off and fly like the wind.

There is a method of catching a wild horse, that may appear to many "a traveller's story." It is called *creasing* a horse. The meaning of the term is unknown to me.* It consists in shooting a

---

* *Creasing* may be derived from *craze,* or the French *écraser,* or the Teutonic *krossa,* or the English *crush,* to bruise, overwhelm, or subdue without killing. It may be Spanish; for it is said that the modern South Americans practise the same devise. It would

horse in the neck with a single ball so as to graze his neck bone, and not cut the pith of it. This stuns the horse and he falls to the ground, but he recovers again, and is as well as ever, all but a little soreness in the neck, which soon gets well. But in his short state of stupefaction, the hunter runs up, and twists a noose around the skin of his nose, and then secures him with a thong of buffalo-hide. I do not give it merely as a story related ; but I believe it, however improbable it may appear, because I saw it done. I saw an admirable marksman, young Andrew Sublet, fire at a fine horse, and after he fell, treat him in the way I have mentioned ; and he brought the horse into camp, and it turned out to be a very fine one. The marvel of the story is, that the dextrous marksman shall shoot so precisely as only to graze the vital part; and yet those who know these matters better than I do, say, that they conceive it possible.

After we had made peace with the large body of the Black-foot Indians, for, as we may say, a *quid* of tobacco, nothing occurred worth relating until we arrived at the town of Independence, being the first white settlement in our way homewards. I would, however, here remark, that the warlike body just mentioned, though of the fierce Black-foot tribe, hunted and fought independently of that troop with which we had a battle in the Rocky Mountains ; and were most probably ignorant of that affair, in which a chief was treacherously shot by one Antoine, who was half Indian and half French, when bearing a white flag, and with which

---

seem as if it jarred the vertebræ, or bony channel of the neck without cutting any important vessel or nerve. But let the fact be established before we reason upon it.

nefarious deed I believe Captain Sublet had no concern. But of all this I cannot speak with certainty, as I myself was half a mile distant, when the Black-foot chief was shot, and his scarlet robe torn off of him by the mongrel Indian, as a trophy instead of his scalp; for the Indians returned their fire so promptly, and continued fighting so long, even after dark, that there was no time nor opportunity of his securing that evidence of his savage blood and mode of warfare.

When we arrived at the town of Independence, Dr. Jacob Wyeth, Palmer, Styles, and myself bought a canoe, being tired of travelling by land, and impatient to get on, and this was the last of my money except a single six-cent piece. A thick fog prevented our early departure, as it would be dangerous to proceed on account of the snags and sawyers in the river. To pass away the tedious time, I strolled out around the town, and lost my direct way back. At length the fog cleared off, and after my companions had waited for me an hour, they pushed off and left me behind! They, be sure, left word that they would wait for me at the next town, Boonsville, twenty miles distance. I hurried, however, as fast as I could five miles down the banks of the river; when, finding that I could not overtake them, and being fatigued by running, I gave over the chase in despair. I was sadly perplexed, and vexed, at what I conceived worse than savage usage. In this state of mind, I saw a small skiff, with a pair of oars, when an heroic idea came into my half-crazed brain, and feeling my absolute necessities, I acted like certain ancient and some modern heroes, and jumped into the boat, cast off her painter, and pulled away for dear life down the stream.

The owner of the boat discovered me when not much more than a quarter of a mile on my way. He and another man got into a canoe and rowed after me, and gained upon me; on perceiving which, I laid out all my strength, and although two to one, I distanced them, and they soon saw they could not overtake me. When I started it was twelve o'clock, and I got to the next town, Boonsville, the sun half an hour high, — the distance about twenty miles. When my skiff struck the shore my pursuers were about twenty rods behind me. I ran into the first barn of a tavern I could reach. They soon raised the neighbors, and placed a watch around the barn, one side of which opened into a cornfield. In searching for me they more than once trod over me, but the thickness of the hay prevented them from feeling me. I knew the severe effects of their laws, by which those who were too poor to pay the fine were to atone for their poverty by stripes, which were reckoned to be worth a dollar a stripe in that cheap country; and hence I lay snug in the hay two nights and one day without any thing to eat. Hunger at length forced me from my hiding-place, when I went into the tavern, where I found Dr. Jacob Wyeth, Walter Palmer, and Styles. I told the landlord I was starving for want of food, and he gave me supper; and then I went back into the barn again, where I slept that night.

The next morning I went into the tavern again, and there I found my pursuers, and they found their prisoner, whom they soon put under the custody of two constables, who ordered me breakfast, which having eaten with a good relish, I watched my opportunity, while they were standing thick around the bar, and crept unobserved out of the back-door into the extensive cornfield, and thence into the barn window out of which they threw manure, and regained my snug hiding-hole, where I remained one day and one night more. I now and then could see the constables and their *posse* prowling about the barn, through a crevice in the boards. In the midst of my fears, I was amused with the solemn, and concernful phizes of the two constables, and one or two others. In the morning very early, I ventured out again, and ran down to the river; and there spying a boat, and feeling heroic, I jumped into her and pushed across the river, and landed on the opposite bank, so as to elude the pursuit of the authorities, who I knew would be after me on the right bank of the river, while I marched on the left. When I came to the ferry near St. Louis, I had only a six-cent piece, which the ferryman took for his full fare which was twelve cents, and so I got safe to St. Louis, but with scarcely clothing enough for decency, not to mention comfort: and yet I kept up a good heart, and never once despaired. My companions arrived a day before me; they on Thursday, I on Friday, at four o'clock in the afternoon; they in the steam-boat, like gentlemen, while I, the youngest in the whole Oregon company, like a runaway. But I do not regret the difference, seeing I have a story worth telling, and worth hearing.

Where to get a lodging that night I did not know, nor where to obtain a morsel of bread. I went up to a large tavern, and asked permission of the keeper to lodge in his barn that night, but he sternly refused. I then went to the other tavern, and made the like request, when the landlord granted it, saying that he never refused a man sleeping in his barn who was too poor to pay for a lodging in his house. I wish I knew his name. I turned in and had a very good night's rest. Should any one enquire how I came to leave my old companions, and they me, I need only say that I had a very serious quarrel with one of them, even to blows; and with that one too who ought to have been the last to treat me with neglect; "and further the deponent saith not."

The next morning I went round in search of work, but no one seemed disposed to hire me; nor do I much wonder at it; for in truth I was so ragged and dirty, that I had nothing to recommend me; and I suffered more depression of spirits during the following six days of my sojourn at St. Louis, than in any part of my route. The steam-boats refused me and Dr. Wyeth started off for New Orleans before I could see him. Palmer let himself by the month on board a steam-boat running between St. Louis and Independence, while I was left alone at the former place six days without employ, victuals, or decent clothing. I could not bear to go to people's doors to beg; but I went on board steam-boats and begged for food. I was such a picture of wretchedness that I did not wonder they refused to hire me. My dress was buck-skin moccasins, and pantaloons; the remains of a shirt I put on in the Rocky Mountains, the remnants of a kersey waistcoat which I had worn ever since I left Cambridge, and a hat I had worn all the time from Boston, but without any coat whatever, or socks, or stockings; and to add to the wretchedness of my appearance, I was very dirty, and I could not help it. My looks drew the attention of a great many spectators. I thought very hard of it then, but I have since reflected, and must say that when people saw a strong young man of eighteen in high health, and yet so miserable in appearance, it was natural in them to conclude that he must be some criminal escaped from justice, or some vagabond suffering under the just effects of his own crimes.

At length, wearied out by my ill forture, I plucked up courage, and went to the Constitution steam-boat, Captain Tufts, of Charlestown, near Boston, and told him my name and family ; and detailed to him my sufferings, and said that he *must* give me a passage, and I would work for it. To my great joy he consented, and he gave me shirt, pantaloons, &c. ; and I acted as *a fireman,* or one who feeds the fire with pine wood under the steam-boilers. I forbear narrating the particulars of my sufferings for want of food during the six days I tarried at St. Louis. Suffice it to say, that I was in a condition of starvation, and all owing to my wretched appearance. When I at times went on board the steam-boats, I was glad to scrape up any thing after the sailors and firemen had done eating. At length I obtained employ in the steamboat Constitution, and a passage to New-Orleans, on the condition of acting as one of the firemen, there being twelve in all, with five men as sailors, and two hundred and forty passengers, partly emigrants, but chiefly men belonging to the settlements on the Mississippi, going down to Natchez, and to New-Orleans to work. We tarried one night at the Natchez ; but soon after we left it the *cholera* broke out among the passengers, eighty of whom died before we reached New-Orleans, and two of our own firemen. A most shocking scene followed.

I felt discouraged. My miseries seemed endless. After trying day after day in vain to get a passage in a steam-boat, I was made happy in procuring one, though I paid for it, by working as a fireman, the hardest and most disagreeable occupation on board; still I was contented, as I had victuals enough to eat; and yet, after all, I saw men perishing every minute about me, and thrown into the river like so many dead hogs. It is an unexaggerated fact that I witnessed more misery in the space of eight months than most old men experience in a long life.

On arriving at New-Orleans, Captain Tufts sent off every man of the passengers, leaving those only who belonged to the boat. He gave me shirts and other clothing, and offered me twenty dollars a month, if I would go back to St. Louis with him. I remained on board about a week; and so desirous was I to get home, that I preferred going ashore, although I knew that the yellow fever and black vomit, as well as cholera were committing great havoc in the city. The shops, stores, taverns, and even the *gambling-houses*, were shut up, and people were dying in-doors, and out of doors, much faster than they could be buried. More white people were seized with it than black; but when the latter were attacked, more died than the former. The negroes sunk under the disorder at once. When a negro gets very sick, he loses all his spirits, and refuses all remedies. He wishes to die, and it is no wonder, if he believes that he shall go into a pleasant country where there are no white men or women.

I soon got full employ as a grave-digger, at two dollars a day, and could have got twice that sum had I been informed of the true state of things. In the first three days we dug a separate grave for each person ; but we soon found that we could not clear the hearses and carts. I counted eighty-seven dead bodies uninterred on the ground. Yet where I worked, was only one of the three grave-yards belonging to the city, and the other two were larger. We therefore began on a new plan. There were twenty-five of us grave-diggers. We dug a trench fifty-seven feet long, eight feet wide, and four feet deep, and laid them as compactly as we could, and filled up the vacant spaces with children. It was an awful piece of business. In this large trench we buried about, perhaps, three hundred ; and this business we carried on about a month. During this time, you might traverse the streets of New-Orleans, without meeting a single person, except those belonging to the hearses, and carts, loaded with the dead. Men were picked up in the morning who died after dark before they could reach their own houses. If you ask me if they died with yellow fever, or cholera, I must answer that I cannot tell. Some said the one, and some the other. Every thing was confusion. If a negro was sent by his master to a carpenter, for what they called a coffin, which was only a rough board box, he was commonly robbed of it before he got home. I myself saw an assault of this kind, when the poor black slave was knocked down, and the rude coffin taken from him. New-Orleans is a dreadful place in the eyes of a New-England man. They keep Sunday as we in Boston keep the 4th of July, or any other day of merriment and frolic. It is also a training day every other Sunday for their military companies.

I was in part witness to a shocking sight at the marine hospital, where had been many patients with the yellow fever. When the doctors, and those who had the care of that establishment had deserted the house, between twenty-five and thirty dead bodies were left in it; and these were so offensive from putrefaction, that when the city corporation heard of it, they ordered the house, together with the bodies to be burnt up; but this was not strictly complied with. A number of negro slaves were employed to remove the bodies, which being covered with wood and other combustibles, were all consumed together.

At length I was attacked myself with symptoms of the yellow fever, — violent pain in my head, back, and stomach. I lived at that time in the family of a Frenchman, who, among his various occupations, pretended to skill in physic. He fed me on castor oil. I took in one day four wine-glasses of it, which required as much resolution as I was master of: but my doctor assured me that he had repeatedly scared away the yellow fever at the beginning of it, by large and often repeated doses of that medicine. Its operation was not one way, but every way. I thought I should have no insides left to go home with. Yet is it a fact, and I record it with pleasure, that it carried off all my dreadful symptoms, and in a very few days, I had nothing to complain of but weakness, which a good appetite soon cured. I therefore recommend a man in the first stage of yellow fever to take down a gill of castor oil, made as hot as he can swallow it; and repeat the dose in eight hours.

I remained nine weeks in New-Orleans, a city so unlike Boston, in point of neatness, order, and good government, that I do not wonder at its character for unhealthiness. Stagnant water remains in the streets as green as grass, with a steam rising out of it that may be smelt at the distance of half a mile. Beside this, their population is so mixed, that they appear running against each other in the streets, every one having a different object and a different complexion. In one thing they seem to be agreed, and to concur in the same object, namely, *gaming*. In that delirious pursuit, they all speak the same language, and appear to run down the same road to ruin.

I am glad that it is in my power to support what I have said respecting the Marine Hospital, by the following public testimony, published by authority, taken from one of their newspapers.

"NEW-ORLEANS.—The following report from a committe appointed to examine one of the hospitals, will account, in some degree, for the unprecedented mortality which has afflicted New-Orleans. The report is addressed to the mayor.

" The undersigned, standing committee named by the city council during the prevalence of the epidemic now desolating the city, have the honor to report, that, in consequence of information given by sundry respectable persons, relative to the condition of the hospital kept by Dr. M'Farlane, they repaired to-day, at half-past one o'clock, to said hospital; that in all the apartments they found the most disgusting filth; that all the night *vessels* were full, and that the patients have all declared that for a long time they had received no kind of succour; that in many of the apartments of the building they found corpses, several of which had been a number of days in putrefaction; that thence they repaired to a chamber adjoining the kitchen, where they found the body of a negro, which had been a long time dead, in a most offensive state. They finally went to another apartment opposite the kitchen, which was equally filthy with the other rooms, and that they there found many corpses of persons a long time dead; that in a bed, between others, they found a man dying, stretched upon the body of a man many days dead.

" Finally, they declare that it is impossible for one to form an idea of what they have witnessed, without he had himself seen it ; that it is indispensably necessary for the patients to evacuate this hospital, and above all, to watch lest the corpses in a state of putrefaction occasion pestilence in that quarter, and perhaps in the whole city.

" *November* 7. The standing committee has the honor to present the following additional report.

" In one of the apartments where were many living and dead bodies, they found under a bed a dead body partly eaten, whose belly and entrails lay upon the floor. It exhaled a most pestiferous odor. In a little closet upon the gallery there were two dead bodies, one of which lay flat upon the floor, and the other had his feet upon the floor and his back upon the bed forming a curve ; the belly prodigiously swelled and the thighs green. Under a shed in the yard was the dead body of a negro, off which a fowl was picking worms. The number of corpses amounted to twelve or fourteen.

" Signed,   E. A. CANNON, *Chairman.*

       FELIX LABATUT,

             Alderman, Second Ward.

       CHARLES LEE,

             Alderman, First Ward."

I took passage in the ship Henry Thomson, Captain Williams, and arrived in Boston, January 2d, 1833, after an absence of ten months, having experienced in that time a variety of hardships.

CONCLUDING REFLECTIONS.

THE lesson to be collected from this short history is the great danger in *making haste to be rich*, instead of relying upon patient industry, which never fails to give a man his just deserts. Making haste to become rich is the most fruitful source of the calamities of life; for here cunning, contrivance, and circumvention, take the place of diligence. After the schemer's plans have all failed, there seems only one tempting means left to obtain riches in a hurry, and that is by gaming, the most prosperous invention ever devised by the arch enemy of mankind; and when that fails, the next downward step to destruction, excepting drunkenness, is robbery, many instances of which we find recorded in the annals of Newgate and the records of the Old Bailey in London. Such atrocities have never, or very rarely, occurred in our own country, and never will so long as we are wisely contented with the fruits of patient industry, and so long as we believe that the diligent hand maketh rich. These reflections refer to extreme cases, and are not applicable, or meant to be personally applicable, to the unfortunate expedition in which we have been concerned. It is not meant to reprehend those enormous vices and crimes which are known in the old countries, but only to correct a spirit of discontent in men well situated and circumstanced. "*If you stand well, stand still,*" says the Italian proverb.

Some may say this doctrine, if put in practice, would check all enterprise. Not entirely so, provided the means and the end were cautiously adjusted. Christopher Columbus ran a great risk;

yet he knew, from the reasonings of his capacious mind, that there must be "another and a better world" than that he was born in; and under that strong and irresistible impression he tempted the trackless ocean and found it. But what shall we say of our Oregon adventurers, who set out to pass over the Rocky Mountains, and thence down the Columbia river to the Pacific ocean, in boats upon wheels? and that too with a heavy load of goods, and those chiefly of iron. What renders the project more surprising is, that they should take with them the most ponderous articles of a blacksmith's shop, — anvils, and a large vice. It is more than probable that the old and long established wholesale Indian traders at St. Louis laughed in their sleeves, when they saw such a cargo fresh from the city of " *notions*," paraded with all the characteristic confidence of the unwavering Yankee spirit. After assuring them that their ingenious and well-constructed amphibious vehicles would not answer for travelling in such a rough country as they must go through, they purchased all three of them, and advised our leader to buy sheep and oxen to live on between the white settlements and the country of the savages, and not to trust to their guns for food. This turned out very wholesome advice, as they must have starved without that provision.

The party under Captains Lewis and Clarke, sent out by the government of the United States, consisted of nine young men from Kentucky, four teen soldiers of the United States army who volunteered their services, two French watermen, — an interpreter and hunter, — and a black servant belonging to Captain Clarke. All these, except the last, were enlisted to serve as privates during the expedition, and three sergeants were appointed from amongst them by the captains. In addition to these, were engaged a corporal and six soldiers, and nine watermen, to accompany the expedition as far as the Mandan nation, in order to assist in carrying the stores, or repelling an attack, which was most to be apprehended between Wood river and that tribe. This select party embarked on board three boats. One was a keel-boat fifty-five feet long, drawing three feet of water, with a large square sail, and twenty-two oars, with a forecastle and cabin, while the middle was covered by lockers, which might be raised so as to form a breast-work. There were beside two *periogues*, or open boats of seven oars each. They had two horses, for any purpose, which they led along the banks; and fourteen bales of goods, with a variety of clothing, working utensils, locks, flints, ammunition, and richly-laced coats, and other gay dresses, and a variety of ornaments suited to the taste of the Indians, together with knives, flags, tomahawks, and medals. Yet all these articles were exhausted, without any accident or particular loss. The party was led by two experienced military officers, and the men were under military regulations; which was not the case with the Cambridge adventurers, who were upon shares, and all on a level.

We are unwilling that our readers should rely entirely on our opinion of the inadequacy of the outfits for such a formidable undertaking as that of going from the Atlantic shore of New-England to the shore of the Pacific by land. We shall therefore subjoin the opinion of a sensible gentleman, who had spent some time in the Missouri territory, and traversed its dreary prairies, where no tree appears, and where there is, during the greater part of the year, no fuel for cooking, nor water fit to drink. He says : " Do the Oregon emigrants seek a fine country on the Oregon river? They will pass through lands [to get to it] of which they may buy two hundred acres for less than the farther expenses of their journey." * He tells us that a gentleman (Mr. Kelly) has been employing his leisure in devising schemes to better the condition of his fellow countrymen, and has issued advertisements, inviting the good people of New-England to leave their homes, their connexions, and the comforts of civilized society, and follow him across the continent to the shores of the Pacific. He tells those who may reach St. Louis, that they will find there many who have been to Oregon, and found no temptation to remain there; — that they may possibly charter a steamboat from St. Louis to the mouth of the river Platte, but no farther, as that stream is not navigable for steamboats unless during freshets. And after they reach the mouth of the Platte, they will have a *thousand* miles to go before they reach the Rocky Mountains; and the country through which the adventurers must pass is a level plain, where the eye seeks in vain for a tree or a shrub, — that in some places they must travel days and nights without finding wood or water, for that the streams only are scantily fringed with wood. Our Cambridge emigrants actually found this to be the case, as they had no other fuel for cooking their live stock than buffalo-dung. The writer says, (and he had been there,) that the ground is covered with

*See New-England Magazine for February and April, 1832, under the signature of W. J. S.

herbage for a few weeks in the year only, and that
this is owing to the Indians burning the Prairies
regularly twice a year, which occasions them to be
as bare of vegetation as the deserts of Arabia. The
same experienced traveller assures them that they
could not take provisions with them sufficient for
their wants, and that a dependence on their guns
for support was fallacious, and the same uncertainty
as to the buffaloes ; — that sometimes those animals
were plenty enough, and sometimes more than
enough, so as to be dangerous. When they trot
smartly off, ten thousand and more in a drove, they
are as irresistible as a mountain-torrent, and would
tread into nothing a larger body than the Cambridge
fortune-hunters. Their flesh is coarse beef, and
the grisly bear's, coarse pork ; but this kind of bear,
called the *horrible* from his strength and ferocity, is
a most terrific beast, and more disposed and able
to feed on the hunter than the huntsman upon
him. We can assure the emigrants, says the writer
already quoted, from our own experience, that not
one horse in five can perform a journey of a thousand miles, without a constant supply of something
better than prairie-grass.

The journal of Lewis and Clarke to the Pacific
ocean, over the Rocky Mountains, was a popular
book in the hands of every body ; and the Expedition of Major Long and company was as much read ;
and both of these works detail events and facts
enough, one would suppose, to deter men from such
an arduous enterprise ; not to mention the hostile
tribes of Indians through which they must pass. It
seems strange, but it is true, that a theoretical man
need not despair of making the multitude believe
any thing but truth. They believed the enthusiastic

Mr. Hall J. Kelley, who had never been in the Oregon territory, or seen the Rocky Mountains, or a prairie-dog, or a drove of buffaloes, and who in fact knew nothing of the country beyond some guess-work maps ; yet they would not read, consider, or trust to the faithful records of those officers who had been sent by the government to explore the country and make report of it.

There is a passage in the essay written by W. J. S. which we shall insert here on his authority, as it cannot be supposed that we, at this distance, should be so well acquainted with the affairs in Missouri, as one who had resided on the spot. We assume not to keep pace with the professed eulogist of Oregon, of its river, and its territory, its mild climate, its exuberant soil, and its boisterous Pacific, so inviting to the distressed poor in the neighbour-hood of Boston ; who are exhorted by him to pluck up stakes and courage, and march over the Rocky Mountains to wealth, ease, and independence. The passage we allude to reads thus : — " About twelve years since, it was discovered by a public-spirited citizen of St. Louis, that the supply of furs was not equal to the demand. To remedy this evil, he raised a corps of sharp-shooters, equipped them with guns, ammunition, steel-traps, and horses, and sent them into the wilderness to teach the Indians that their right was only a right of occupancy. They did the savages irreparable injury. They frightened the buffaloes from their usual haunts, — destroyed the fur-clad animals, and did more mischief than we have room to relate." He adds, sarcastically, that " the Indians were wont to hunt in a slovenly manner, leaving a few animals yearly for breeding. But that the white hunters were more thorough-spirited, and made root-and-branch work of it. When they settled on a district, they destroyed the old and young alike ; and when they left it, they left no living thing behind them.   The first party proving successful, more were fitted out, and every successive year has seen several armed and mounted bands of hunters, from twenty to a hundred men and more in each, pouring into the Indian hunting grounds ; and *all this has been done in open and direct violation of a law of the United States, which expressly forbids trapping and hunting on Indian lands.*   The consequence has been that there are now few fur-clad animals this side the mountains."

Lewis and Clarke, and some other travellers, speak of friendly Indians, — of their kindness and hospitality, and expatiate on their amiable disposition, and relate instances of it.   Yet after all, this Indian friendship is very like the affection of the negroes in the Southern States for their masters and mistresses, and for their children, — the offspring merely of fear.   There can be no friendship where there is such a disparity of condition.   As to their presents, an Indian gift is proverbial.   They never give without expecting double in return.

What right have we to fit out armed expeditions, and enter the long occupied country of the natives, to destroy their game, not for subsistence, but for their skins?   They are a contented people, and do not want our aid to make them happier.   We prate of civilizing and Christianizing the savages.   What have we done for their benefit?   We have carried among them *rum, powder* and *ball*, small-pox, starvation, and misery.   What is the reason that Congress, — the great council of the nation, — the collected wisdom of these United States, has turned a deaf ear to all applications for establishing a colony on the Oregon river? Some of the members of that honorable house of legislation know that the district in question is a boisterous and inclement region, with less to eat, less to warm the traveller, and to cook with, than at the mouth of any other known river in the United States. We deem the mouth of the river St. Lawrence as eligible a spot for a settlement of peltry merchants as the mouth of the Columbia. When Lewis and Clarke were on that river, they had not a single fair day in two months. They were drenched with rain day and night; and what added to their comfortless condition was the incessant high winds, which drove the waves furiously into the Columbia river with the tide; and on its ebb, raised such commotion, and such a chopping sea, that the travellers dared not venture upon it in their boats; yet the Indians did, and managed their canoes with a dexterity which the explorers greatly admired, but could not imitate. The boisterous Pacific was among the new discoveries of our American adventurers. Had their expedition been to the warm climate of Africa, or to South America, they would have been sure of plenty to eat; but in the western region, between the Rocky Mountains and the great river of the West, the case is far otherwise.

It is devoutly to be wished that truth may prevail respecting those distant regions. Indeed the sacred cause of humanity calls loudly on its votaries to disabuse the people dwelling on these Atlantic shores respecting the Oregon paradise, lest our farmers' sons and young mechanics should, in every sense of the phrase, stray from home, and go they know not whither, — to seek they know not what.

Or must Truth wait on the Rocky Mountains until some Indian historian, — some future *Clavigero** shall publish his annals, and separate facts from fiction? We esteem the " *History of the Expedition under the command of Captains Lewis and Clarke to the Sources of the Missouri, thence across the Rocky Mountains, and down to the Pacific Ocean,*" substantially correct. Their conduct towards the Indians was marked throughout with justice and humanity; and the journal of that ex-' pedition will be a lasting monument of their judicious perseverance, and of the wisdom of the government of the United States.

Reader! The book you have in your hands is not written for your amusement merely, or to fill up an idle hour, but for your instruction, — particularly to warn young farmers and mechanics not to leave a certainty for an uncertainty, and straggle away over a sixth part of the globe, in search of what they leave behind them at home. It is hoped that it may correct that too common opinion that the farther you go from home the surer you are of making your fortune. Agriculture gives to the industrious farmer the riches which he can call his own; while the indefatigable mechanic is sure to acquire a sufficiency, provided he "build not his house too high."

Industry conducted by Prudence is a virtue of so diffusive a nature that it mixes with all our concerns. No business can be managed and accomplished without it. Whatever be a man's calling or way of life, he must, to be happy, be actuated by

---

* The Abbé Clavigero, a native of Vera Cruz, who resided forty years in the Provinces of New Spain, spoke the language of the natives, and has written the History of Mexico.

a spirit of industry, and that will keep him from want, from dishonesty, and from the vice of gambling and lottery-dealing, and its long train of miseries.

The first and most common deviation from sober industry is a desire to roam abroad, or in one word, a feeling of *discontent*, — a making haste to be rich, without the patient means of it. These are reflections general and not particular, as it regards all such high hopes and expectations, as led to our Oregon expedition and to its disappointments. The most that we shall say of it is, — that it was an injudicious scheme arising from want of due information, and the whole conducted by means inadequate to the end in view.

> Oh happy — if he knew his happy state,
> The man, who, free from turmoil and debate,
> Receives his wholesome food from Nature's hand,
> The just return of *cultivated* land.

THE END.